Prototypes

An Anthology of School Improvement Ideas That Work

Selected from the *Phi Delta Kappan*
and updated by
Stanley M. Elam

Phi Delta Kappa Educational Foundation
Bloomington, Indiana

cover design by Carol Bucheri

Library of Congress Catalog Card Number 89-061103
ISBN 0-87367-800-1
Copyright © 1989 by the Phi Delta Kappa Educational Foundation
Bloomington, Indiana

Table of Contents

Introduction

In the spring of 1987 Bob Cole asked me if I thought it would be a good idea for Phi Delta Kappa to publish an anthology of Prototype articles chosen from the *Phi Delta Kappan*. If so, would I edit the book? I said, "Maybe. Let me take a look." (Bob seemed unaware that I don't read the *Kappan* quite as avidly as I did before he succeeded me as *Kappan* editor in January 1981.)

It took me a week — such is the working pace in retirement — to read the 80 or so Prototype pieces published since the fall of 1981. That was the date when Bob changed this department's name from the original "New and Significant." When I had finished reading, I was enthusiastic. Yes, indeed, an anthology of the best of these pieces would be worthwhile. Prototypes, usually relegated to the back pages of the journal, are a treasure trove of worthy ideas and ingenious projects for school improvement. Almost all of them are portable. That is, they can be adopted by any school or education agency looking for answers to particular problems. I said to Bob, "This anthology should be just right for a leadership group like Phi Delta Kappa."

I had one reservation. What if a project, written up by an enthusiastic promoter oblivious to its drawbacks, went down the tubes soon after the glowing *Kappan* account appeared? As we all know, pride of ownership does not guarantee success. Somewhere I have read that fewer than one-third of the innovations introduced in education since 1900 have survived. America's great elder statesman Ralph Tyler has warned "that it takes six or seven years to get a reform really working as intended."* While Prototype projects are generally too modest to qualify as "reforms," many elements are similar. Both require, on the part of the user, a commitment to the best goals of education and a certain amount of nerve, a willingness

---

*See "Education Reforms," *Phi Delta Kappan* (December 1987): 277-80.

to put one's reputation on the line. They often require hard work and long hours. They take imagination combined with patience and persistence. And above all, they require leadership. Even when innovators bring these qualities to bear, there are no guarantees. Successful projects are dropped in times of financial austerity. The politics of education kills others. Time after time, a program withers when its parents change jobs.

In any case, I determined to check the current health of every program or project reported in this anthology. It was a gratifying exercise. First I selected 50 articles that met my own rather loose criteria: a project had to promise early payoff; it should appeal to a wide range of practitioners; it should be portable; it should be described in enough detail to permit replication; and it should apply primarily to K-12, not post-secondary education. By mail and telephone, I contacted authors or school officials willing to update Prototype reports. I was able to get responses in 45 of the 50 cases. In all but five instances, the programs and projects were alive and well, although a few had been considerably modified, expanded, or contracted. In two cases, projects I considered excellent had been discontinued for reasons having nothing to do with their value; these have been included.

There is something in this book for every progressive educator. These programs and projects do not add up to a major reform of education. They are not highly theoretical. But they have proven valuable in the crucible of practice. They are worth studying and, in many cases, adapting to your own circumstances.

The ideas offered in these pages are so varied, fresh, and original that it is difficult to categorize them under conventional headings. Nevertheless, David Ruetschlin, staff associate in Special Publications at Phi Delta Kappa, has devised five umbrella categories: Keeping Kids in School; Beyond the Classroom: Community Involvement; Staff Development with a Difference; Something Special for Students; and Fresh Curriculum and Teaching Strategies. His categories are helpful, but my advice is this: If you are looking for school improvement ideas in this volume, skim all of the contributions. You are in for some pleasant surprises.

Stanley Elam
15 January 1988

2

Keeping Kids in School

One Community's Response to the Dropout Problem

by Genevieve H. Arnold and Vicki Biggers (May 1987)

While school systems and communities point accusing fingers at one another and try to assign blame for the rising number of school dropouts, one community in the mountains of North Carolina has stopped squabbling and started doing something about the problem. The citizens of Erwin, a suburb of Asheville, have agreed that school dropouts are the responsibility of the whole community and have joined forces with the staff of Erwin Middle School to combat the high dropout rate.

Members of the staff of Erwin Middle School, a part of the Buncombe County School System, decided in 1982 that too many students in the county were not completing high school. The staff decided to create a dropout prevention program that focused on students in grades 6, 7, and 8 who could be identified as at risk of dropping out. The staff believed that early intervention could keep some of these youngsters in school.

The Erwin Middle School staff analyzed the population of the school's attendance area and identified the following factors as possible contributors to the community's high dropout rate.

- Forty percent of the student body were economically disadvantaged.
- Three low-income housing projects were located in the school district.
- Erwin Middle School had the highest rate of referral to court counseling services in the school system.

Ninety-five students from a school population of approximately 1,000 were identified as potential dropouts. These students were failing courses, had excessively high rates of absenteeism, were frequently suspended (either

Genevieve H. Arnold is an assistant professor of education at the University of North Carolina in Asheville. Vicki Biggers is a guidance counselor at Erwin Middle School in Asheville.

in school or out of school), or had high rates of involvement with the juvenile courts.

The school staff decided that, to address the problem properly, the entire community would have to become involved. Consequently, staff members discussed the dropout prevention idea with various youth-related agencies, with women's groups, with court counselors, with school board members, and with the parent/teacher organization. Eventually, this effort led to a comprehensive program designed to meet the academic, social, and emotional needs of high-risk students.

The program planners decided to seek funds to employ a part-time staff member to design and organize the activities of the dropout prevention program. In the first year, the program was financed by state funds earmarked for minors involved with the courts and by matching funds contributed by the local Junior League and the Erwin Optimist Club. In the second year, the program was supported by state funds, matched by local school system dollars. Sources of future funding were to include private foundations, local businesses, clubs, education groups, and state crime-prevention funds.

The program leader was employed initially for 10 months. Her contract was later extended to 12 months so that she could provide year-round support to the students and their families.

The program includes four main components: academic support, parent training and involvement, community service, and case management. The program leader works with teachers and guidance counselors to design an academic support plan for each student. These plans include such activities as group sessions on study skills as well as individual tutoring. The program leader also works directly with the families of participants in their homes and plans seminars on parenting for small groups of parents.

In addition, the program leader coordinates the involvement of community service agencies and local businesses. She develops community service projects for students, such as creating a nature trail, cleaning up river banks and vacant lots, or planning a community garden for the summer months. From local businesses and county agencies, she solicits work contracts for cleanup projects and donations of goods and services. One local business contributed a van to transport students.

Approximately 75 students have been directly served by the program. Students can refer themselves or other students to the program; teachers, parents, and community agencies also can make referrals. However, student participation is voluntary.

Since its inception, the dropout prevention program has yielded the following results.

5

- Court referrals for participants under court supervision have decreased by 60%.
- School attendance has increased by 40% for program participants.
- In-school suspensions of participants have decreased by 50%.
- Training sessions on parenting skills have attracted 40% of the participants' parents.
- The cumulative grade-point average of program participants rose from 1.38 to 1.70.

These statistics attest to the success of the Erwin dropout prevention program. The main strengths of the program are the year-round assistance and support it offers, both in school and out of school, to at-risk students. Although the program requires coordinated and detailed planning, Erwin Middle School and the Erwin community have shown that it is a workable way of reducing the dropout rate.

Update – *Ms. Arnold writes that the targeted intervention program described in this article, now in its fifth year, is flourishing. The program at Erwin Middle School in Asheville currently (1987) serves 65 students. One other school, the Enka Middle School, has replicated the program exactly. Erwin High School has adopted it with minor modifications. The* Kappan *article brought a number of requests for more information and data.*

School and Parents Take Failing Students in Tow in Mandatory Extra-Help Program

by Robert A. Borich (June 1983)

How do you get capable students who are in danger of failing back on the right track? The search for an answer to that perennial school question has led administrators at Rich South High School in Richton Park, Illinois, to adopt a system of mandatory extra-help sessions to compel students to face up to their poor study habits. The program, called Positive Action to Scholastic Success (PASS), is aimed at students with average or above-average ability who are in danger of failing because of poor study habits or motivational problems.

The idea for PASS came from a study conducted by Leroy Eicken, assistant principal for pupil personnel services. In response to teachers' concerns about underachieving students, Eicken focused on 26 students of average or above-average ability who were nonetheless failing a total of 60 classes. He administered a questionnaire to these students and to their teachers. The results revealed two main causes of failure: incomplete or missed daily assignments and students' failure to make up these missed assignments. Other reasons rated high by teachers (but not by students) were inattentiveness in class and failure to take notes. Using the information from Eicken's survey, Donald Trimble, the principal of Rich South, and his administrative staff obtained the approval of Superintendent James Warren and of the district executive council to design an extra-help program.

This program is scheduled for the first 45 minutes after the end of the regular school day, and it takes precedence over all other activities. Once a student is assigned to PASS extra-help sessions, no other school activity − not even athletics − can be used as a legitimate excuse for absence from the sessions.

Students may be assigned to PASS extra-help sessions by only one teacher at a time. (Occasionally students have actually assigned themselves to the

---

Robert A. Borich is director of informational services for the Rich Township High Schools, Park Forest, Ill.

7

program.) When a teacher assigns a student to the PASS sessions, the teacher fills out a form that lists pertinent data, including time, place, and frequency of the sessions and what work needs to be done. The student is expected to continue attending the sessions until his or her classwork is judged to be passing. Copies of the PASS form go to the guidance office, the teacher, the student, and his or her parents.

The involvement of parents is central to the success of the program. Parents are told why their children have been assigned to PASS and the importance of attending the sessions. If a student misses a scheduled session without offering a legitimate excuse, he or she is referred to the pupil personnel office, which then contacts the parents a second time. Those students who miss PASS sessions repeatedly will be dropped from the class whose teacher initially assigned them to the program. Only two students were dropped from classes during the first two years of the program. School officials attribute this record to strong parental support for and cooperation with the program.

The school administration is especially careful to emphasize the positive and remedial aspects of the program and to discourage the use of extra-help sessions as punishment. According to Trimble, the chief goal of PASS is to help students learn that regular study habits pay off in classroom success.

Figures compiled after the first year of operation seem to support the administration's belief that the program has reduced the number of course failures and increased students' self-confidence. One-third fewer students were assigned to the PASS program during the second semester. Assuming that the teachers continued to believe in the program, this reduction suggests that the number of potentially failing students has diminished. Moreover, the number of failing grades received by PASS students during the second semester declined by 50%. School officials feel that this is a significant decrease, even taking into account the smaller number of students in the PASS program during the second semester.

Of the 31 teachers who assigned students to PASS during the first year, 28 rated their experience with the program as either excellent, very good, or good. The few who did not like the program cited extra paperwork for teachers and the "spoon-feeding" of high school students as objectionable features of the program.

The problem of extra paperwork for teachers is handled by a clerical staff member who keeps records and processes forms. The PASS clerk confers periodically with each student assigned to the program to assess that student's satisfaction with his or her own progress. The teacher also comments on student progress on a follow-up report issued by the clerk. Conflicts and lack of progress are handled by the director of pupil personnel services in a conference with the student.

The administration feels that, while the PASS program puts pressure on the underachieving student, it also recognizes that some students need more direction than others and takes into account the wide range of motivation and maturity among students. A great advantage of the program, according to Trimble, is that it sends a clear message to the parents that education is a responsibility that they must share with the school. The PASS program shows that the school is interested in the classroom performance of students and asks parents to join in the effort.

Update — *In November 1987 Mr. Borich described the program's success as follows:*

Now in its seventh year, Rich South High School's PASS program continues to be used by teachers to get failing students back on track. Some 114 students (out of 1,300) have been placed in PASS during the first semester — 69 following the first grade report of the year. Only 15 of those have failed to show up so far for the after-school sessions.

Principal Donald Trimble says PASS works because it involves the parents and eliminates students' excuses for not getting their school work done. Trimble says PASS has wide support in the school community because it makes completion of school work a top priority, something teachers and parents agree is essential to success in school. "We have never had a parent who has not supported putting his or her child into the after-school program," he says.

Assistant Principal Leroy Eicken says, "The same 15 to 20 teachers are regularly assigning students to PASS, and some teachers have never used it. But gradually more teachers are filling out the form and calling the parent."

A School District Fights the Battle of Truancy with Some Success

by James L. Hanson and Douglas L. Hoeft (February 1983)

For most educators the word truancy means failure — failure for students, parents, teachers, and administrators. In an effort to reduce this failure, the 160 schools in the Kane County (Illinois) Educational Service Region established the Kane County Truancy Prevention Program in 1976.

Kane County schools enroll some 71,000 K-12 students from both rural and urban communities. During the last 15 years district attendance had been falling at an annual rate of 0.1%, from 95% in the early 1960s to 93.51% in 1975. Therefore, the district undertook a number of studies to investigate the truancy problem and to help direct the efforts of the fledgling Truancy Prevention Program.

To determine the relationship between truancy and completing school, the district studied the records of 240 truants, from the time their pattern of truancy began until they reached the age of 20. Only seven of these students (2.9%) graduated from high school; none passed the GED exam for a high school equivalency diploma.

The district also studied 407 truants to see how their attendance rate varied during the course of a school year. As the year progressed, the students' truancy rate accelerated from an average autumn rate of 19.5% to an average spring rate of 27.6%. In addition, if these students returned to school the following year, they started at the truancy rate they had reached the previous spring.

Several studies explored the connection between truancy and trouble with the law. One of the studies traced 127 truants from three separate towns

---

At the time this article was written in 1983, James L. Hanson was superintendent of the Kane County Educational Service Region, Geneva, Ill., where Douglas L. Hoeft was assistant regional superintendent and director of the Kane County Truancy Prevention Program. Since then, Hoeft has succeeded James Hanson, who retired.

for a period of two years. At the end of that time, 76% of these truants had records with the legal system.

The district also studied the records of 55 students who were petitioned into the local juvenile court system during an 18-month period. Before they were petitioned into court, these students were truant, on the average, 47% of the time. After they had been placed under the direction of a probation officer, they were truant 63% of the time.

The adult court system, working with the parents of truants, fared somewhat better. Sixty-five students who were petitioned into adult court had been truant, on the average, 36.3% of the time. After their parents appeared before the judge, their truancy rate fell to 21.1%.

The Kane County Truancy Prevention Program operates on four levels to help truant students: 1) through the local schools, 2) through the regional truancy prevention office, 3) through the community social service agencies, and 4) through the courts. The program combines counseling with the real threat of significant negative consequences. For example, if a child and his or her family do not accept counseling and the child remains truant, the district takes legal action.

Staff members at each school are expected to exhaust all local resources before referring a student to the district truancy prevention office. When local efforts fail, an administrator petitions the Truancy Prevention Program, which assigns the case to one of three youth outreach workers. Within 24 hours, the outreach worker contacts the student, in school or at home, and tries to determine the cause of the truancy. At the same time a strongly worded legal notice is sent to the student's parents, advising them of their legal responsibility to see that their child attends school. Should the efforts of the outreach worker fail or should a complex family problem be discovered, the student and his or her parents are referred to an adult family counselor, whose job is to secure the aid of appropriate community service agencies.

If the truancy problem persists, a certified letter is sent to the parents, directing them to attend a conference at the Truancy Prevention Program office in the county courthouse. At this conference, the full extent of the school attendance law is explained to the parents; and a contract is drawn up, requiring each of the parties − the district and the parents − to take specific action to deal with the child's attendance problem. At the end of the conference, the parents are served with a formal legal notice.

If a child is still not attending school regularly after all of these steps have been taken, the case is referred to court. This step generally requires the parents to make several court appearances. If the parents choose to hire an attorney, their legal fees are likely to be more costly than the fine that the court will impose. By the end of the 1981-82 school year, the district had won 48 of 50 cases that had gone to trial during that year. The parents had been fined from $25 to $500 and had been ordered to jail for up to 30 days.

But the proper aim of a truancy prevention program is not winning court cases and sending parents to jail; the aim is to keep more children in school for more days per year. During the first five years of the Kane County project (the years for which figures are available), an average of 674 cases were sent to the central program office each year. Of these, an average of only 177 a year went as far as the truancy conference and an average of only 66 cases a year ended up in court. Some 90% of all cases were controlled before court action became necessary.

The program also has kept more children in school for more days. In every year since 1976, the average attendance rate for Kane County schools has been better than that for the state of Illinois, and the gap has been widening. Thus the 1.04% difference in favor of Kane County schools during the 1980-81 school year (see Table 1) means that, on a normal school day, 738 more students were attending classes in the county than would have been predicted by the statewide average. At the same time, the dropout rate at Kane County secondary schools has been improving. The annual number of high school dropouts in the county has fallen from a high of 1,839 in 1978 (a 6.03% annual rate) to 1,253 in 1981 (a 4.53% annual rate).

Table 1. Average Daily Attendance, Kane County/State of Illinois

	1975-76 Before Program	1976-77 First Year	1977-78 Second Year	1978-79 Third Year	1979-80 Fourth Year	1980-81 Fifth Year
Kane County	93.51	93.64	93.16	93.19	93.51	93.93
State of Illinois	93.02	92.88	92.29	92.24	92.47	92.89
Difference	+.49	+.76	+.87	+.95	+1.04	+1.04

The effect of these additional students on the local school budget is not negligible. In Illinois, as in many other states, the financial aid formula for schools is based on average daily attendance. The local districts in the Kane County region receive approximately $5 per student attendance day. Thus, for those 738 additional students, Kane County schools received $664,000 more than expected over the course of a 180-day school year.

The annual budget for the Truancy Prevention Program during that same year was only $140,000.

The Truancy Prevention Program offers parents a choice: working with counselors (through the school or through community service agencies) or facing the legal system. Most choose the former option. Our multilevel strategy contributes to the success of the program by providing as many chances as possible to solve truants' problems and bring them back to school. No single administrator, counselor, or case worker is charged with the full responsibility of changing the behavior of all truants. Professionals working at each level of the program solve a portion of the problems; only a few are ultimately referred to the courts.

For years educators have maintained that investing time and effort in truancy prevention is wasteful, because such efforts produce few tangible results. Judging from our experience in Kane County, that need not be the case. A properly run truancy prevention program can be a valuable and cost-effective asset to any school system.

Update — *Mr. Hoeft writes that Kane County is still using the same intervention system described here. In 1986 the Illinois State Board of Education ranked the Kane County program first among the 40 truancy prevention programs funded by the state. What worked when this article was written still works.*

Last year the Kane County region's 68,000 students had a 94.65% attendance level, the highest since the early 1960s. The number of dropouts has followed the same favorable trend, moving down from 1,823 to 1,144, a 37% decrease. Although the attendance level in the entire state of Illinois has improved over the past decade, the Kane County record is at least one percentage point better.

Hoeft believes that much of the credit for the improved state record should go to the Illinois State Board's Truancy Prevention Program. The Kane County model has been adopted to a greater or lesser degree by most of the service regions in Illinois, he says.

A Promising Approach to Absenteeism in the Secondary School

by Lee C. Malbon and Ronald L. Nuttall (September 1982)

Students are absent for three major reasons: illness, weather and transportation problems, and personal choice. Illness produces a rate of absenteeism that averages 4% to 5% annually.[1] Weather and transportation problems keep an additional 2% of students out of school. Thus a rate of absenteeism that averages 6% to 7% seems reasonable. But rates of absenteeism of 10% to 15% are not uncommon today, and in inner-city schools they can sometimes be even higher.

Prior to the 1977-78 school year, student attendance had become a major concern in Malden, Massachusetts. Both the high school faculty and the administration recognized that administrative practices were not dealing effectively with attendance problems.

During the 1976-77 school year, 42,097 student absences (representing 12.6% of total student days per year) and 4,654 student requests for early dismissal indicated that many youngsters saw regular attendance as unimportant. The three- and four-day school week were becoming common among students who felt no sense of involvement in or commitment to their own education.

The attendance policy at that time required students who were absent from one or more classes without permission to make up time in after-school detention. Three unexcused absences were cause for a two-day suspension, and the assistant principal held a conference with the offending student's parents before he or she could return to school. There was no penalty for frequent excused absences.

In an attempt to improve school attendance, the Malden School Committee endorsed a new high school attendance policy for the 1977-78 school

Lee C. Malbon is assistant principal of Burrillville Junior/Senior High School in Harrisville, R.I. Ronald L. Nuttall is a professor and director of the Laboratory for Statistical and Policy Research at Boston College, Chestnut Hill, Mass.

year, intended to place responsibility for school attendance on students and their parents. The major change in the attendance policy was the institution of a mandatory failing grade of E for the seventh unexcused absence per quarter in each subject. Excused absences for school-sponsored activities, religious holidays, emergencies, and prolonged illness under a doctor's care did not count toward the six allowed absences per subject each quarter.

This policy is quite lenient. Beyond monitoring truancy, the administration makes no attempt to determine how students spend the days they miss. Moreover, if a student were to use all the allowed unexcused absences for four quarters, he or she could avoid any mandatory E's and still show an attendance rate of only 87%.

The school mails written reports from classroom teachers notifying parents of a student's third, sixth, and seventh absence. With the seventh unexcused absence, a student automatically receives a failing grade of E in that subject for that quarter. At the teacher's discretion, depending on the work that a student has completed, the value of the E to his or her yearly average may range from 0 to 59 percentage points of the 100 points for a given quarter.

Students may appeal to a review board for exceptions to the attendance policy. This board consists of the assistant principal, a teacher elected by the faculty, two students from the Student/Faculty/Administration Advisory Board, and the guidance counselor assigned to a student who appeals. The two student members may be excluded at the petitioner's request.

One drawback of the new attendance policy is the increased clerical burden. Teachers must maintain accurate records on an authorized form for each class. They must complete the official notifications that are sent to parents and students after the third, sixth, and seventh absences. And they must submit to the assistant principal at the end of each quarter a list of students who are to receive a mandatory grade of E.

The clerical tasks of the assistant principal have multiplied as well. A copy of each notification form sent home by teachers must be filed with the assistant principal. In addition, the assistant principal arranges parent/teacher conferences to discuss attendance, verifies absences for illness under a physician's care, compiles a schoolwide list of students who have accumulated unexcused absences, and sits as a member of the review board.

Guidance counselors also provide additional support services under the new plan. They receive copies of the notification forms sent to parents and arrange conferences with students to discuss attendance. The counselors also sit on the review board. Meanwhile, the typing, distribution, and mailing required by the new attendance policy have become added duties for the high school office staff.

Increased clerical burdens seem a small price to pay for the success of the new attendance policy. Student attendance at Malden High School increased by 3.7% for the entire population of 2,100 students — from 87.4% in 1976-77 to 91.1% in 1977-78. The improvement in attendance represented an average of six additional school days per student. Moreover, the winter of 1978 was the harshest in New England in recent memory; the improvement in attendance might have been even greater had the weather been less severe.

The new attendance policy had the greatest impact on low-achieving students, who also tend to have the highest absentee rates. We divided into achievement groups the class of 1977, which was totally under the old policy, and the class of 1978, which went through the policy change between its junior and senior years. Achievement categories, derived from students' junior-year grades, were: B+, B, C+, C, D+, D, and "other." Those students in the last category were usually failing.

Figure 1 shows the improvement in days of school attended for students in these two classes from their junior to their senior years. The overall attendance for both classes improved in the senior year. The class of 1977, under the old attendance policy, improved by an average of 1.6 days; the class of 1978 improved by an average of 2.8 days — 1.2 days more than the class of 1977.

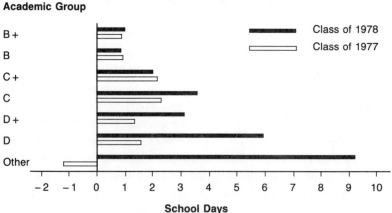

Figure 1. Additional School Days in Attendance, by Academic Group

Figure 1 also shows that, for the class of 1978, the increase in days present was concentrated among those students with the lowest overall achievement levels. Thus the "other" group, whose members had achievement levels below a grade of D, gained 9.2 days under the new policy. In the class of 1977, by contrast, these low-achieving students actually lost an average of 1.2 days of school from their junior to their senior years. Similarly, the D students in the class of 1978 gained an average of 5.9 school days as seniors, while those in the class of 1977 gained only 1.6 days.

At the end of its first year, the Malden attendance policy had reduced the overall absentee rate. And the greatest reduction in absenteeism occurred among the lowest achievers — those most likely to be voluntarily absent.

---

1. Scott Thomas and David Stanard, "Attendance and Absenteeism," *The Practitioner*, March 1975, pp. 1-12.

Update — *Since writing this article with Mr. Nuttall, Mr. Malbon has instituted a similar approach to the problem of absenteeism at Burrillville Junior/Senior High School, Harrisville, R.I. Results have been gratifying there also.*

Beyond the Classroom: Community Involvement

Changing the Generation Gap to a Gain: The Grandpeople Program

by **Judith L. Endeman** (November 1985)

An often overlooked resource for the schools is the retired segment of the community. By the year 2000, one-third of the citizens of the United States will be over 60 years old. Most will be retired, yet still healthy, energetic, and with a lifetime of experience to offer. Mobilizing this group to support public education can be an exhilarating experience.

Two schools in Poway, California, have successfully tapped the rich resources of these retired citizens to supplement and improve their educational programs through the Grandpeople Volunteer Program. At Westwood Elementary School and Twin Peaks Middle School, more than 100 "grandpeople" volunteer their time each week. The services they provide include: 1) acting as one-on-one tutors in the reading program, 2) staffing the library circulation desk and shelving and cataloging library books, 3) assisting in science labs, as students learn to use microscopes and Bunsen burners, 4) supervising the kitchen during a cooking class, 5) drilling students with math flash cards, and 6) being primary resources for an eighth-grade oral history project.

The key to a successful grandpeople program is the selection of a capable, energetic individual as its coordinator. A retired educator who understands educational programs and has an interest in and enthusiasm for people is the type of person to fill this position. And a retired person who must minimize income in order to retain retirement benefits usually is willing to work as a part-time consultant at a bargain rate.

The coordinator meets with each teacher in order to discuss his or her specific needs for volunteer assistance in the classroom. Questions the coordinator might ask include: What type of help is needed? How many volun-

---

At the time this article was written in 1985, Judith L. Endeman was principal of Twin Peaks Middle School, Poway, Calif. She now is assistant superintendent for instruction and planning in the Ramona (Calif.) Unified School District.

teers will this require? With what academic area should the volunteers be familiar? What time will you need the volunteers?

Once this initial survey of the schools' need for volunteers has been conducted, the coordinator spends the next few weeks vigorously recruiting volunteers at senior citizens centers, attending breakfast and luncheon meetings of local service groups, and announcing the need for grandpeople volunteers at local churches and synagogues. The coordinator also distributes fliers containing information about the program and posters depicting the activities of those already involved in the program.

Potential volunteers are invited to visit the school. The coordinator takes them on a tour of the building; and at the conclusion of the tour, volunteers' skills and interests are matched with school needs. This matching is crucial to the program's success, but it is not carved in stone. If, for any reason, any participant − teacher, student, or volunteer − is uncomfortable with a match, another can be arranged.

A survey conducted in the spring of 1984 by Bob Gilchrist, coordinator of the program at Twin Peaks Middle School, attests to the success of the program. Thirty-six of the 42 teachers surveyed indicated that the grandpeople volunteers had been "very helpful" to them. Only three reported that they were "not so helpful," while three stated that the value of the program was much more than academic learning. Teachers also cited as benefits of the program "improved respect for the elderly" among the students, "improved self-esteem of students," and "motivation of elderly to support public schools."

The volunteers benefit from their involvement in the program, as well. It provides an outlet for their talents and energies and allows the elderly to stay involved in society and help shape the future through positive interaction with and influence on young people.

The oft-mentioned "generation gap" can become a "gain" to the schools as oldsters meet youngsters. Those who have the experience of the past may be the solution to meeting the challenge of the future for education in America.

Update − *By 1987 the Grandpeople Volunteer Program in the Poway schools was stronger than ever, writes Judith Endeman.*

Partly because of the strong community component of the volunteer program, Twin Peaks was selected in 1984 as one of the National School Recognition Program's outstanding middle schools. Two years later the school became one of the first California Distinguished Middle Schools. In both awards, the Grandpeople Volunteer Program was cited as an example of *how a school can use rich community resources without excessive cost. Only a part-time coordinator is needed to manage and build the program. This person is hired as a consultant for $3,000 to $4,000 per year. This minimal investment may bring the benefit of 3,600 hours of volunteer time to the school.*

As a consultant, the coordinator can arrange his or her work responsibilities around personal and vacation schedules. Several months at the beginning of the year are needed to advertise the program and arrange the teacher-retiree matches. The coordinator may work daily for several weeks, then work half-days for a month. Once the program is operational, he or she may only need to visit the school once or twice a week.

Beyond the consultant fee for the coordinator, there are minimal costs. Recognition teas put on by homemaking classes, invitations and certificates created by art classes, and plaques from the shop consume $200 to $300 worth of materials. Specially purchased badges for the volunteers make them feel important and official. A small-group room or office and access to a phone are helpful.

The Twin Peaks program has recently been expanded. First, with cooperation and funding from a local Kiwanis Club, a videotape was prepared to recruit and introduce new volunteers to the program. With this and a slide presentation showing seniors working with youngsters, the coordinator finds it easier to interest new seniors in the program.

Another new component of the program is called the "mystery guest speaker." This appeals to those who cannot commit to a regular schedule of volunteering but want to be of service to the school. The coordinator arranges for guest speakers, who bring symbols and tools of their work into sixth-grade classes. Through a 20-question format, the students guess the speaker's occupation. This process focuses the students' attention on the speaker and teaches them to improve both questioning and reasoning skills. A range of specialists, from space-age technicians to candy store owners, tell students why education is important and what kinds of skills and training they will need for success in the world of work.

Ms. Endeman notes that something similar to the Grandpeople Volunteer Program in Poway is being introduced in Ramona, where she now works. Through the Adopt-a-School program, a senior citizens club had, as of December 1987, adopted an elementary school. Little by little, tutoring matches were being made. The School Site Council was considering whether to finance a coordinator in order to expand the program.

Meeting Students' Need to Serve

by Timothy B. Evers (December 1986)

The community service internship at East Lyme (Connecticut) High School helps students understand the needs of various segments of the local population and allows them to engage in community service for a substantial period. Established in the spring of 1985, the Community Service Internship (CSI) is the only credit-bearing course of its kind to be offered by a public school in Connecticut and one of only a handful of such courses in the United States.

The CSI curriculum was developed by a committee of high school administrators and teachers, under the direction of Assistant Superintendent Mary Jo Kramer. The internship is designed to foster an understanding of societal issues on both an experiential and an academic level.

The academic component of the community service internship covers the problems of hunger, poverty, housing, education, health, aging, and handicaps — dealing with each from historical, political, economic, and social/cultural perspectives. The service component engages each student in an internship with one of 22 local agencies. Students spend a minimum of 2½ hours each week working at these agencies in non-clerical capacities.

During the second week of the course, representatives of the 22 agencies attend an "agency fair," at which they talk to students and answer their questions. During the third week of the course, each student is scheduled for an on-site interview at one of the three agencies for which the student has specified a preference. The options range from working in special education or English-as-a-second-language programs to working with physically or mentally handicapped young adults or with the elderly.

The academic component of the internship takes up one class period each day. Initially, the students spend this time discussing their interests and abilities and the types of services rendered by the participating agencies. Once students have been placed with agencies, however, two class meetings each

---

Timothy B. Evers is a guidance counselor at East Lyme (Conn.) High School.

23

week focus on societal issues. During these sessions, students discuss newspaper or journal articles and films, listen to lectures by the teacher or by guest speakers, and take part in workshops on human relations and on communication skills. One class period each week is devoted to discussing students' internship experiences at the individual agencies. During the remaining two periods each week, students work independently on supplemental readings, research projects, journal entries about their community service experiences, oral reports, and final projects. The final grade for the course is based in equal measure on a student's performance in the internship and on classroom performance.

Meeting at the close of the 1984-85 school year to evaluate the new program, the planning committee concluded that most of its goals had been met. After completing the course, students seemed to display greater empathy, sensitivity, tolerance, and understanding toward individuals who were different from themselves. The planning committee also judged both the academic component and the service component of the internship as highly effective.

However, the service component of the pilot program offered problems as well as rewards. Administering the student internships was sometimes made more difficult by a lack of communication with the agencies. For example, students were not notified on several occasions that an activity had been canceled until they arrived at the site. Moreover, the contact people at the agencies were not always in charge of supervising the interns' performance and sometimes failed to return phone calls and to submit final evaluations of their interns.

Yet the students agreed that the service component was the "most beneficial" part of the course. Several interns put in more than the minimum amount of time required, and two students (who were not old enough to obtain summer jobs) continued to work with their agencies during the summer vacation. Another student, who had been apprehensive about the experiential portion of the course, became one of its most ardent advocates. In her evaluation of the program, she said that working with a child who had severe physical handicaps made her feel "wanted and needed." Still another student, who tutored a younger teenager, noted that "helping others and letting them know people care" gave him a "warm feeling."

All 12 students who enrolled in the first year of the internship participated in a school assembly aimed at recruiting other students for the program. The principal also presented the 12 with certificates of appreciation for their service to the community. Three students volunteered to share their internship experiences with the board of education at a meeting in early

June 1985. Local newspapers were kept apprised of program developments, from the planning stage during the summer of 1984 through the evaluation one year later.

The community service internship became part of the regular curriculum at East Lyme High School when the board of education funded the one-semester course for the 1985-86 school year. The number of students enrolled in the course rose to 15 during the second year. Three other course sections, funded with seed money from the Bodenwein Public Benevolent Foundation, gave other students opportunities to receive academic credit for community service, as well.

The planning committee made three significant changes in the community service internship course for the second year. To alleviate the communication problem with certain agencies, a new job description was written for the program coordinator, giving that teacher more time (the equivalent of teaching one course) for contacts with agencies, on-site visits, and record keeping. To add variety to the presentation of course materials and to give the course an interdisciplinary, collaborative quality, two teachers from different departments are teaching the four sections. A teacher from a third department was selected to serve as coordinator. Finally, an advisory committee composed of community leaders, parents, teachers, and students now works with the planning committee to insure that the course remains responsive to changing agency and community needs.

In *High School*, Ernest Boyer recommended that community service be required of all high school students. However, the planning committee believes that such a requirement contradicts the fundamental principle of volunteerism. As a compromise, the community service internship has been incorporated into the social studies program at East Lyme High School. In addition to completing credits in world history and American history, students must select one course in the area of human needs. The community service internship is one social studies elective that fulfills that requirement.

Some questions with important implications remain to be answered. For example, can the community service internship be adapted effectively for students in middle school or in junior high school? Would a similar program be appropriate for inclusion in the elementary school curriculum? The committee structure now in place in East Lyme insures that such questions will not only be raised, but also answered — by the schools and the community together.

Update — *The community service internship (CSI) has undergone a number of changes since publication of this article, Mr. Evers writes. Students* *now are able to choose internships at 27 different community agencies, and participants have added individual as well as small-group internship projects, such as changing storm windows and raking leaves for elderly residents who live alone.*

The East Lyme Board of Education is now the sole source of funds for the program. Although the 1987 supply budget of $540 was half the 1985-86 budget, the school board's allocation for each of the past two years has doubled. The course now is taught by a teacher from one department (science) who also is the program coordinator. This person receives an additional stipend but no extra time. Lack of communication between the school and the agencies, noted in the original article, remains a problem.

Approximately 20 students continue to elect CSI each year and are enthusiastic about the uniqueness of the internship experience. The CSI Advisory Committee members believe enrollment would increase if the present non-departmental course were included as an elective within the social studies department, a recommendation that may be considered.

Thus CSI is still in flux. Questions concerning the adaptation of community service at the middle and elementary schools in East Lyme will be addressed when developmental problems of the course at the high school are resolved. Mr. Evers welcomes inquiries.

Improving Community Relations Through Business and University Cooperation

by Roger N. Grabinski (April 1984)

In 1977 the Chamber of Commerce of Mount Pleasant, Michigan, and Central Michigan University took a significant step toward maintaining good relations between the community and the university. The Chamber/University Business Education Services Committee (CUBES) was created to serve as a liaison between the local business community and the university and to stimulate the exchange of information and services between them. CUBES comprises an approximately equal number of chamber members who work for the university and chamber members who work in private enterprise.

Good community relations have always been important to the university, because a healthy community environment makes it easier to attract high-quality faculty members and students to the campus. Members of the business community, for their part, have long understood the significance of the boost given the local economy in the form of university salaries and the money that students spend in the community. The university is crucial to the success of businesses in Mount Pleasant, because the university is the largest employer in the town and the surrounding area is largely rural.

Before 1982, the committee had looked to its own members to come up with program ideas and most often sought out well-known consultants from outside the community to provide the desired programs. This method produced one or two notable successes, but there also were some failures. After a time, the committee began to run out of ideas and attempted fewer and fewer programs.

In 1982, however, CUBES decided to broaden its focus. Instead of keeping all responsibility for generating programs strictly within its own member-

---

Roger N. Grabinski is chairperson of the CUBES committee and is also responsible for the Community Leadership Program in the Department of Counseling, Educational Administration, and Community Leadership at Central Michigan University, Mount Pleasant. *CUBES: The Seminar Process*, a detailed description of the programs described here, is available for $5 from the Mount Pleasant Area Chamber of Commerce, 300 E. Broadway, Mount Pleasant, MI 48858.

ship, the committee decided to share that responsibility with the more than 900 university faculty members and administrators. The committee first identified a few topic areas that seemed likely to be interesting to the business community and sent a request for proposals to all full- and part-time faculty members and middle- and upper-level university administrators. Where CUBES had had difficulty identifying successful program ideas in the two preceding years, the committee was suddenly very busy evaluating several excellent program proposals. Moreover, the programs did not come solely from the University School of Business, which was typically the route through which the business community approached the university. Proposals came from such departments as home economics, educational administration, counseling, speech and drama, and psychology.

Successful seminar programs were held in 1982 on the topics of investments, sales, effective advertising, and employee selection and supervision. All of these programs were presented by faculty members from Central Michigan University. In 1983 the chamber sponsored successful programs on time management, stress, personal health maintenance, and the effect of new tax laws on restaurants.

CUBES considers a program to be a success if it breaks even financially. The cost of running a program includes a token honorarium for the presenter. Usually this honorarium is in the form of a small sum of cash or an appropriate gift; the size of the honorarium varies according to the nature of the presentation. A faculty member who leads a panel discussion receives a smaller honorarium than one who provides a three-hour lecture/discussion seminar.

The seminars have proved to be an effective means of sharing university resources with the community, and the program will be continued. At the same time, the committee is attempting to channel resources in the other direction, from the business community to the instructional programs of the university. During the spring of 1983, chamber members were asked to provide information about their business and personal expertise and to indicate whether they would be willing to meet with classes, talk informally with students, or share their information in some other way. CUBES then compiled a *Business Resource Guide* and distributed it to all university faculty members in the winter of 1984. The form requesting information also offered any business person who wished to take part in a university program a chance to learn how to organize material and to be more effective in presenting it to a group.

Support for CUBES from the university and the chamber of commerce has been excellent. The president of Central Michigan University has made available to the committee such campus services as mail delivery and copying, and the chamber has increased the amount of working capital available for the committee. In addition, the Department of Counseling, Educational Administration, and Community Leadership has been supportive in a variety of ways, and each of the four schools within the university provided financial support for the publication of the *Business Resource Guide*.

The realization that the university is a rich source of information that can be mined by the local business community revitalized the committee and made it a powerful vehicle for public relations, both for the chamber and for the university. CUBES is now functioning as a bridge between the local business community and the university, and the total community is much the better for it.

Update – *Mr. Grabinski writes that few would question that the program described in this 1984 article was and continues to be very successful in increasing understanding and cooperation between the university and the community. It is difficult, however, to present hard data to support this statement because of the complex nature of community interactions. When programs like CUBES get started, they stimulate other initiatives; and, of course, many efforts that preceded the formation of the seminar program continue.*

Some things have changed and some have remained the same since the article appeared. Seminars of the same type and frequency still are offered jointly by the Chamber of Commerce and the university; however, the structure through which the seminars are delivered has changed. The joint Chamber/University Business Education Service Committee (CUBES) has evolved into the Business Education Committee of the Chamber of Commerce. Like the former CUBES committee, it is comprised of chamber members from the private sector and from the university. This committee works with a new economic development corporation created and jointly maintained through contributions from the university and the business community.

Another important change is that the proposal process for generating program ideas is not used now. That process was an excellent way of getting things started and involving a large number of people. On the other hand, it is more labor intensive and requires more time than more traditional approaches. A major reason it was used in the first place was that the traditional approaches were not working. When the methods of organization currently used begin to be ineffective, the proposal method will almost certainly be resurrected to stimulate new vitality.

Publication of this article stimulated at least 50 requests from colleges and universities throughout the United States for the complete set of descriptive materials. An additional 50 or more have been picked up from the Chamber of Commerce office in Mount Pleasant by visitors or local people for their own use or to send to colleagues.

Teacher Fair: Counterpoint to Criticism

by Sara Ingrassia (April 1983)

Public school teachers are under attack. Many of them ask, How do we counter the demoralizing and often unfair criticisms of our classroom techniques and capabilities? How do we point out the many and varied successes we achieve with our students? How do we show the public that teachers do teach and that students do learn?

Teachers in Rockford, Illinois, responded to these questions in May of 1981 with a teacher fair. What better way to get the message across to the media, the taxpayers, the parents — even the teachers themselves — than to move the classroom and its products into the marketplace? And what better marketplace than the largest shopping mall in the Rockford school district?

Envision, if you will, a two-story shopping mall stretching the length of two city blocks. This mall is filled with displays of students' work: research papers, fiction and poetry, yearbooks, newspapers, sculpture, paintings, industrial arts and home economics projects, science and history projects. Students and teachers stand nearby, eager to talk about the work on view. In the center court of the mall, jazz bands, choirs, orchestras, and groups of thespians entertain shoppers nonstop.

An elementary classroom has been re-created in one corner of the first floor, complete with desks, chalkboard, and visual aids. Throughout the weekend, teachers who have volunteered for this assignment teach actual lessons to their students in this classroom — a math lesson for fifth-graders, a batik lesson for some special education students, a lesson on playing musical instruments for a class of kindergartners. A high school classroom has been re-created on the second floor of the mall, where model lessons in the secondary disciplines are taught.

Sara Ingrassia is a fourth-grade teacher in Kishwaukee Elementary School and manager of Counterpoint to Criticism, a project of the Rockford (Ill.) Education Association, with funding from the National Education Association through a Hilda Maehling Fellowship for 1982-83.

31

Off in another area of the mall, teams of students from the five Rockford high schools are competing in a "Quiz Bowl." The questions have come from the 9-12 curriculum. Crowds of parents and shoppers cheer on their favorite teams — proof that academic contests can be as exciting as athletic ones.

Staff and students of the Area Vo-Tech Center have taken over one wing of the mall for demonstrations of skills related to cooking, auto repair, child care, drafting, and practical nursing. Other sections of the mall feature demonstrations by staff and students in special education, bilingual education, and alternative programs.

Some 44,000 people visited the Rockford mall during the weekend of the teacher fair. They couldn't help but be impressed by both the quantity and the quality of the programs that the public schools were offering to the children of the community. They couldn't help but be impressed by the energy, the talent, and the creativity of the 400 teachers whose instructional efforts had yielded these displays. They had to sense the pride and accomplishment that hundreds of students felt as they showed their abilities.

A teacher fair is a microcosm of a school system — at least, of that part of a system where teachers and youngsters work together on activities intended to promote learning. Of course, the microcosm can be expanded to give the public a look at district support services or even at administrative services. The Rockford fair included these elements. But the emphasis always remained on the teachers and on their students. The primary goals were to provide a showcase for students' talents and accomplishments and to re-create the excitement and fun of the best of their academic, artistic, vocational, and imaginative activities in the classroom.

A teacher fair is a positive and honest response to negative criticisms of the schools. A teacher fair does not deny the weaknesses of U.S. public education. Instead, it provides on-the-spot, three-dimensional demonstrations in living color of the strengths of public education.

A teacher fair is a morale booster for teachers, both those who participate and those who observe. Here the accomplishments of district classrooms are publicly displayed and acknowledged. Moreover, such a fair enables both teachers and the public to experience the educational system as a whole, from kindergarten through grade 12.

A teacher fair also spotlights students' academic accomplishments and gives them recognition. Finally, a teacher fair is a project on which teachers and administrators can cooperate positively, creatively, and enthusiastically.

A teacher fair is a celebration of the successes of public education — an opportunity for a community to take a firsthand look at its school system in action. What better way to counter criticism?

Planning a Teacher Fair

The teacher fair in Rockford, Illinois, was one year in the planning — from May 1980, when the idea was first proposed, to May 1981, when the idea became a reality. Teacher organizations in other districts that would like to hold similar fairs may find the Rockford planning schedule helpful.

1. *May 1980:* Decide to do it — and to do it big.

2. *September 1980:* Establish a strong steering committee; members should have leadership skills, organizational ability, energy, enthusiasm, and a talent for getting along well with others.

3. *September 1980:* From among the members of the steering committee, choose a project manager who gets along well with the district administration.

4. *September 1980:* Reserve the largest shopping mall in the school district for a weekend in early spring.

5. *October 1980:* Present your plans for the fair to the district superintendent and solicit his or her support; these plans should cover such things as publicity, necessary materials, and potential sources of funding.

6. *November 1980 — January 1981:* Present the idea to the district teaching staff through fliers, announcements at staff meetings, or personal contacts.

7. *February 1981:* Hold several well-publicized sign-up meetings for would-be participants.

8. *March 1981:* Meet with mall and school district officials to line up available materials and to establish guidelines for their use, storage, and transportation to and from the mall.

9. *March 1981:* Schedule participants and assign them spaces in the mall and specific times to appear.

10. *April 1981:* Begin publicity campaign.

11. *April 1981:* Arrange for classroom substitutes for the fair manager and for one helper, so that they can take care of preliminary arrangements on the day before the fair and take care of loose ends on the day after the fair.

12. *May 1981:* Hold the fair.

13. *May 1981:* Send notes of appreciation to those individuals whose contributions helped to make the fair a success.

14. *May 1981:* Evaluate the fair.

Update — *Rockford teachers have not repeated the successful fair described in this article. Ms. Ingrassia says she is not sure exactly why, but suggests that the concerns that led teachers in the early Eighties to sponsor such fairs have greatly diminished. The major motivation behind the*

Rockford fairs was to spotlight the variety of demands placed on teachers and the success with which teachers were meeting those demands, despite a great deal of negative media coverage of education. Today criticism seems to be aimed primarily at administrators and school boards, Ms. Ingrassia says. So Rockford teachers, at least, have not felt the need to justify their professionalism, certainly not on such a large scale as a K-12 teacher fair. Also, the Rockford Teachers Association leadership has had other priorities.

Ms. Ingrassia notes that she was invited to help the large school districts of Portland, Oregon, and Des Moines, Iowa, sponsor fairs similar to those held in Rockford.

The School/Community Survey:
A Useful Tool in Improving Education

by Terri V. Hunt, Marla J. Weatherl, and
Deborah A. Verstegen (June 1986)

The public opinion poll is a tool often used to sample the political convictions of large groups of people. But, as members of the Foundations in Educational Administration (FEA) Program at the University of Texas, Austin, have discovered, such surveys also can be useful in improving public education locally. Unlike such national polls as the annual Gallup education poll, a local school/community survey provides school officials with a direct indication of the opinions of their constituents.

The FEA Program has been in existence since 1952. It is a nine-week, nine-credit-hour course that grooms selected classroom teachers for administrative positions. Applicants accepted into the program receive a stipend to offset their expenses.

Every summer since 1954, students in the FEA Program and their professors have traveled to Texas communities — large and small, urban and rural — to interview residents about their schools. Each year, the FEA class, which numbers approximately 20 students, formulates its own organizational structure for completing the survey. The following steps must be carried out: 1) communicating with the board and superintendent to identify issues of concern, 2) developing a questionnaire, 3) charting a random sampling procedure, 4) collecting the data, 5) analyzing the data, and 6) producing the survey document.

The 1984 survey, conducted in Levelland, Texas, grew from the work of three committees: sample plan/logistics, questionnaire preparation, and

Terri V. Hunt is a third-grade teacher in the Round Rock (Tex.) Independent School District, where Marla J. Weatherl is director of music. Both were students in the Foundations in Educational Administrative Program described in this article. When this article appeared, Deborah A. Verstegen was an assistant professor of educational administration at the University of Texas, Austin, where she directed the Foundations in Educational Administration Program. She is now with the Department of Educational Leadership and Policy Studies, University of Virginia.

35

production. Definition of the sampling areas and basic planning for the trip were handled by the six-member sample plan/logistics committee. Based on population and ethnicity, the district was divided into six rural and 30 urban survey areas. Approximately 30 minutes were allowed for each interview, and every seventh household was chosen to insure a random sample. Both daytime and evening survey sessions were scheduled in order to achieve an adequate sampling of the adult population. The sample plan/logistics committee also developed a detailed itinerary, organized travel groups, and selected survey teams.

The six-member questionnaire-preparation committee developed the initial survey instrument. Using issues outlined by the school board and the superintendent, the committee constructed a 25-item questionnaire and presented it to the entire class for refinement. Because the Levelland district contained a large Hispanic population, the questionnaire also was translated into Spanish. The committee developed a computer program to expedite the tallying of data. Committee members then instructed the rest of the class in the procedures for recording responses.

Transforming raw data into a meaningful form was the task of the production committee. This committee drew up an outline for the completed document, which was to include a historical overview of the community and school district, as well as general information about the methodology of the survey. This committee also designed figures and tables to illustrate the findings. From these, a "mock-up" of the document was prepared. Members of the production committee constructed a flow chart to facilitate the production of the final document.

The 18-member travel group went to Levelland by car on a Tuesday morning. The Levelland Independent School District (LISD) provided housing for the team at South Plains Junior College. Survey headquarters were set up in the LISD board room before the six survey groups began interviewing on Tuesday evening. Interviewing continued through Wednesday and Thursday, with one team of surveyors remaining at headquarters during each survey period to tally responses. On Friday, team members analyzed the results and prepared an 80-page document. A summary of the survey results was presented at a school board meeting that evening. The survey team returned to the university on Saturday morning.

At a time when public school reform has placed greater demands on local districts, the school/community survey can be a useful administrative tool for the improvement of education. The survey has proved itself to be a reliable gauge of public opinion. In addition, the cost and time involved in contracting with a professional polling organization would be many times greater than the expense incurred by a district for a survey conducted by the teachers in the FEA Program. The cost of the FEA school/community survey includes only food, travel, and lodging for the group. The school/community survey is useful to those who conduct it, as well. The activity makes future administrators aware of the importance of public opinion to school improvement.

Update — *Ms. Verstegen states that the University of Texas program described here continues without major changes.*

Bangor Township Students Find the Human Connection

by Robert W. Meadows (October 1983)

Each semester, 60 eighth-grade social studies students from Bangor Township (Michigan) Junior High School spend one morning a week working in preschools, in elementary schools, in the public library, and in nursing homes. They are all enrolled in the Social Studies Human Services Program at their school.

The students work person-to-person — no clerical or custodial chores. They read to the elderly, write letters for them, help them with simple exercise programs, talk to them, and listen to them. They play with the preschoolers; lead them through games that use letters, numbers, and color words; and help in dozens of other ways to prepare them for school. At the public library, they lead reading groups and perform hand puppetry. In the elementary schools, they help prepare learning materials and tutor youngsters who are acquiring and practicing new skills.

The program is the brainchild of Nancy Meadows, a teacher of social studies and mathematics at Bangor Junior High, and of Pat Slebiska, a former assistant principal at the school. But taking 60 students into the community once a week over the course of a 13-week semester requires plenty of teamwork. Two administrators, three teaching teammates, a college consultant, and a number of bus drivers join forces at one time or another to plan, inform the parents, prepare the students, transport them to and from the sites, observe their work, read their journals, keep records, and direct the weekly debriefing sessions. Even the superintendent has been pressed into service on occasion, and his station wagon is always commandeered. Fifteen visitation sites have been established, and it takes one school bus and six cars to deliver and pick up the students each Wednesday morning.

Part of the rationale for the program stems from current brain research, which suggests that middle-schoolers might benefit from opportunities to

---

Robert W. Meadows is a professor of education at Saginaw Valley State College, University Center, Mich.

consolidate and apply what they have learned in earlier grades in a variety of new and different settings. But Meadows offers other, perhaps more important, reasons for the program. She explains that the final test of any social studies program is how well it connects youngsters with their community. A maturing person must ask two basic questions: Who am I? What can I do to help others? When young people find constructive answers to these questions, they begin to grow up.

Friendship through service, personal ownership of shared tasks, and growth through self-discipline are the foundation stones on which Meadows and Slebiska built the program. They hoped that students would demonstrate growth in at least five areas: communication, responsibility, cooperation, concern, and self-concept.

The classroom preparations for the visits provide numerous opportunities to practice communication. Activities are focused to sharpen speaking and listening skills and to help students learn to respond quickly to written and oral directions. Students also practice cooperation, helping one another develop teaching materials or rehearse the texts they will read in the nursing homes, the preschools, and the library.

Other preparation periods address such serious questions as: How do you talk to adults when you are not trying to fool them, fend them off, or get something from them? Just what is a person-to-person conversation? What are its purposes and payoffs? At the start most youngsters do not know how to answer these questions, so they examine typical transactions, role-play simple conversations, and brainstorm possibilities. They learn to be alert and to look for such potential subjects for their conversations with the elderly as family pictures on the walls, a piece of handwork, a new hairdo or dressing gown. They also learn how to touch, hug, play with, teach, and delight in small children. Classroom preparations and clinical practice lead the eighth-graders to conclude that — age differences notwithstanding — good communication involves the risk of reaching out and accepting another person.

The Social Studies Human Services Program has added layers of meaning to the so-called factual component of the social studies curriculum as well. For instance, the death of a 97-year-old resident of a nursing home affected some of the students deeply. They wanted more information about the treatment of the elderly in our society and about death and dying — and time to share their feelings with one another. When hard economic times led to the layoffs of their parents, some preschoolers no longer attended school. The middle-schoolers wanted to learn more about unemployment compensation, the economics of nutrition, welfare programs, and a host of related topics. Social studies content began to matter to the students.

The program also has improved the public image of the schools. The parents of the middle-schoolers, the supervisors of the sites they visit, and members of the general community have been pleased with the outcomes.

But the real value of the Human Services Program is that it helps the schools develop the kinds of young people who will make good citizens. Arthur Combs has written that "modern education must produce far more than persons with cognitive skills. It must produce humane individuals, persons who can be relied upon to pull their own weight in our society, who can be counted upon to behave responsibly and cooperatively."* At Bangor Junior High School, the Social Studies Human Services Program is making that human connection.

Update — *Mr. Meadows writes:*

Despite economic problems, teacher contract disputes, declining enrollment, teacher reassignments, and conflicts among school board members, the Human Services Program in the Bangor Township School has continued to flourish, largely because of four basic strengths:

First, it fills the students' need for meaningful community involvement, a need solidly confirmed by research on early adolescent growth and development.

Second, it gives students who have low self-esteem abundant opportunities to develop a feeling of self-worth as caregivers.

Third, it provides many opportunities for students to apply seemingly disconnected classroom learnings to real life.

Fourth, the two teachers who have directed and adapted the program are outstanding educators. This does not mean that the program cannot be replicated elsewhere. The same kind of bright, committed classroom teachers can be found in every school system. What is somewhat more rare is the necessary administrative vision and will.

The most troublesome aspect of the program has been transportation. The lengthening bus route reduces the time students can spend at the site. Less time-consuming approaches are now being studied. A second difficulty has been providing continuous on-site contact by school supervisors. This problem has been lessened by excellent classroom preparation and the competence and helpfulness of the professional supervisors at the sites.

---

*Arthur W. Combs, *Educational Accountability: Beyond Behavioral Objectives* (Washington, D.C.: Association for Supervision and Curriculum Development, 1972), p. 23.

Feedback from students, parents, and site supervisors remains positive, so good in fact that we are now doing a longitudinal study to determine the long-term impact of the program.

Finally, for 1987-88, the schedule was designed, for the first time, to permit all 200 eighth-graders to participate.

This Alabama Study Reaches a New Audience — the Public

by Joseph W. Newman and Howard F. Mahan (March 1984)

Internal and external studies of schools and school systems are common, but few such studies are written for the general public. Recently, however, a group of professors from the University of South Alabama, Mobile College, and Spring Hill College conducted a study of the Mobile County School District expressly for the purpose of informing the public about the state of education in their community.

The schools in Mobile are among the most troubled in the U.S. The per-pupil expenditure is $800 below the national average, and a heated controversy over integrating the schools remains unsettled after 20 years of litigation. Concern for the fate of our troubled schools prompted us to ask 24 colleagues — professors of education and of various disciplines in the arts and sciences — to donate their skills to a project designed to inform the residents of Mobile about conditions in their schools.

With the help of a grant from the Committee for the Humanities in Alabama and with access to the resources of the University of South Alabama, we began an analysis of such general administrative issues as school board politics, student competency testing, integration, and school finance and of such academic programs as foreign languages, the special education sequence, and kindergarten. We asked the committee members in each of these areas to research specific topics, describe the current state of the program or issue, evaluate it in light of pertinent national research, and suggest alternatives for improvement. We also asked that their reports be lively, concise, and as free from jargon as possible. The reports became the chapters of a book titled *The Future of Public Education in Mobile*.

Publication of the book was only the beginning of our work, however. Because we were determined to take our findings to the public, we held

---

Joseph W. Newman is an associate professor in the Department of Educational Leadership and Foundations at the University of South Alabama, Mobile, where Howard F. Mahan is a professor of history.

a press conference to announce the release of the study, and we advertised the book by mail and displayed it in several local bookstores. Most important, the committee members took our message to the public by speaking to Parent/Teacher Associations, business organizations, and civic groups.

On at least one level, our message is highly critical of the local schools. Like many other school systems throughout the U.S., the Mobile schools have gone "back to basics" with a vengeance. Our authors concluded that a narrow interpretation of what is "basic" has greatly impaired teaching and learning in Mobile. Therefore, in our talks with the public, we repeatedly stress the need for higher-order thinking skills throughout the curriculum.

But the primary message of our findings is the surprising conclusion that, "given the way we support our schools financially and otherwise, we have a better system than we deserve." Telling people that they have better schools than they deserve puts much of the responsibility for improving the schools squarely where it belongs — on the people. This conclusion never fails to elicit a response. Some listeners are embarrassed, some are defensive, and some (fortunately) are concerned enough to ask what they can do to help.

The solution our study proposes is as easy to say as it is hard to achieve: Strong financial support at the local level is the key to improved schools. The issue of local financing is crucial in Alabama, where per-pupil expenditures are the lowest in the nation. We explain to our audiences that, while Alabama makes a fair commitment to public education at the state level, local support is totally inadequate, largely because residents of Alabama pay the lowest local property taxes in the U.S. Although the situation will not be quickly or easily resolved, we feel we have achieved a major goal by informing the public of the causes of their school system's woeful financial state.

Our study has been well received by teachers, at least partly because we recognized that the last thing school people want is a group of university professors telling them how to run the schools. To offset such resistance, we asked that the superintendent of the Mobile schools and a representative of the teacher union serve as advisors to the study.

We wanted to assure the people working in the schools that ours was a cooperative mission. Teachers and administrators are tired of taking all the blame for today's troubled schools, particularly in a community such as Mobile, where education is always the subject of much media attention. We acknowledged the problem of teacher competence; but we also explained some of its causes, particularly the difficulty of attracting bright people to a profession that offers low salaries, poor working conditions, and little public respect. Though our study is sometimes sharply critical, most teachers and administrators see it as supportive.

We are equally pleased with the overall public reaction to our study — though at a number of our meetings with local citizens we have encountered sharp criticism. At a meeting of a literary society, for example, we faced tough questions about the soundness of teacher education and the viability of integration as a policy for the 1980s. A presentation to a business service organization sparked a heated debate over "oppressive" taxes for public education and the advantages of private schools.

Speaking to critics of public education may not be as pleasant as addressing enthusiastic supporters, but we see the intensity of these discussions as proof that our study has succeeded. We presented the citizens of our community with the facts about their local schools. Now it is up to them to make some important decisions. The Committee for the Humanities in Alabama is encouraging other professors throughout the state to conduct similar studies in their communities. We hope they will accept this challenge, because we think that the first step toward improving our schools is putting the public back in public education.

Update — *Mr. Newman writes:*

Mr. Mahan and I made appearances to publicize the study described in this 1984 article throughout the 1982-83 and 1983-84 academic years. We were delighted that the Committee for the Humanities in Alabama (CHA), our major source of monetary support, encouraged professors at other institutions to undertake studies with a similar focus. In May 1983 Mr. Mahan and I conducted a well-attended workshop sponsored by CHA for potential grant applicants. CHA encouraged applicants to be innovative and try their own approaches; thus no one exactly duplicated our project with CHA funds. Even so, our success in Mobile made CHA more willing than before to sponsor studies focused on public education.

In October 1983 we presented our study to the Alabama State Council for the Social Studies. Several public school teachers and administrators and several professors from other Alabama colleges and universities expressed interest in conducting studies of their local systems. In November 1983 we presented a seminar on the project to the American Educational Studies Association, the national organization for professors of educational foundations. Once again, we found a receptive audience.

Looking back now, we see a number of our recommendations in place as school system policy. We were sharply critical of Mobile's narrow interpretation of "the basics" and the excessive amount of standardized testing. At the time, we felt we were swimming upstream; but now the system has indeed cut back on its testing program, and it has emphasized more

than just lower-level skills and the three R's. Our frank discussion of racial issues admittedly made some citizens uneasy, but today the system is much closer to settling the Birdie Mae Davis *case, the nation's longest-running school desegregation suit.*

Perhaps most encouraging is the fact that Mobile's business community, which initially reacted with hostility when Mr. Mahan and I suggested raising local property taxes to improve the schools (this was the early 1980s, remember), is now working to persuade voters that a tax increase is essential. Our study paved the way for what the Chamber of Commerce is doing today: trying to convince citizens that the entire community suffers when the public schools suffer. As part of this campaign, the Alabama State Department of Education conducted its own study of the Mobile system in 1986-87. The department's personnel read our study first, and their major conclusion was the same as ours: The fundamental problem in the Mobile County Public Schools is lack of money. The message is finally getting through. We feel we planted seeds that have taken root.

Community Education Division Sponsors Child-Care Programs in Public Schools

by Warren J. Winter (February 1986)

Recent changes in the general economic condition of the U.S. (which have sent many mothers back into the workplace) and a tremendous increase in the number of single-parent families have made child-care programs a necessity for many families. To help families with this problem, the Community Education Division of the Charlottesville, Virginia, Public Schools has sponsored child-care programs during after-school hours since the 1976-77 school year. District-sponsored child-care programs are now available in all six of the district's elementary schools.

From 3 p.m. to 5:30 p.m. each school day, these programs serve a total of 336 children between the ages of 5 and 12. If schools are closed because of bad weather or a holiday, the child-care programs are closed also. On days when teachers are scheduled for inservice training, however, the child-care programs' hours are extended to a full day. These programs are completely self-sustaining; parents pay a fee to cover supplies and staff salaries.

The program at Jackson-Via Elementary School is typical of child-care programs offered by the Charlottesville school district. The Jackson-Via program, which has been in operation since 1976, was the first such program offered by the Charlottesville schools. It has as its goal the provision of after-school recreational and enrichment activities for children.

Children enrolled in the program have access to games, toys, and athletic equipment. Audiovisual materials also are used, especially during periods of bad weather. The Jackson-Via program makes use of the school gymnasium, auditorium, library, and outside playground. Recreational materials and first-aid supplies are kept in a storeroom, which also houses a refrigerator for snacks.

Warren J. Winter is director of instruction for the Isle of Wight County (Va.) Public Schools.

During the 1982-83 school year, the tuition charge for this after-school child-care program was 70 cents per hour, payable two weeks in advance. That figure has since risen to $13 a week for daily participation, in order to keep pace with salary increases for staff members.

The after-school day-care program is part of the Community Education Program at Jackson-Via and is supervised by the school's community education coordinator. A teacher and six aides make up the program staff, and all staff members are under the general supervision of the community education coordinator. Enrollment in the program at Jackson-Via is approximately 75 children, and the student/staff ratio is kept at 15:1.

Tutoring and other volunteer services are available from members of Madison House (a service organization at the University of Virginia) and from the National Honor Society at Charlottesville High School. Tutors and volunteers assist the program staff and interact with the children regularly throughout the year.

The Community Education Division also sponsors a summer child-care program at Jackson-Via. This program begins the week after regular classes end in June and continues through the third week of August. The summer program operates Monday through Friday, from 7:30 a.m. to 5:30 p.m. Because of local school board regulations, the program closes during the week following July 4.

For the summer program, a flat rate of $25 per week is charged for one child, $40 for two siblings, and $60 for three siblings. Payments are due on Monday of each week, regardless of the number of days that a child attends during the week. If a child is absent for an entire week, however, there is no charge.

During the summer, staff members plan such activities as swimming, picnics, and trips to local museums and movies. There is no additional charge for these activities. The children also are encouraged to participate in the summer library program at Jackson-Via. If there is enough interest, the children take classes in music, aerobics, art, and reading appreciation. There is an additional charge for those who participate in these classes to pay the instructors and to buy necessary materials.

The salary of the community education coordinator is paid with funds from the local school board and the state. The salaries of all other staff members in both the after-school program and the summer program come from families' tuition payments. The Charlottesville City Council provided $4,000 for these child-care programs in the 1983-84 school year. In addition, the federal Department of Housing and Urban Development provides $4,000 annually. During the 1985-86 school year, the first year in which all Charlottesville elementary schools have participated in the program, the City Council appropriated $18,000 to fund scholarships for students whose parents cannot afford the fees for after-school child care.

Update — *Mr. Winter writes that during the 1986-87 school year the after-school child-care program in Charlottesville served 425 students. The program at each school is supervised by a site facilitator, a position funded by the school board at the rate of $9.25 per hour with part-time benefits. Aides are paid $4.90 to $5 per hour. Parents now pay $16.50 a week to enroll a child full-time in the program, and an internal scholarship fund is available to provide tuition assistance for families needing financial aid. Students from senior government classes at Charlottesville High School serve as volunteers in the after-school program.*

The summer program operates in five of the six city elementary schools. A flat rate of $37 is charged per week; for two siblings the rate is $70; for three, $103.

The after-school program and the summer program are funded entirely with local money; no state or federal funds are used. Both programs are under the supervision of Selah Rainey, whose position as CLAS/S (Creative Learning After School) coordinator is full-time for 12 months and is funded by the Charlottesville School Board.

Project ABLE: Help for Adults with Learning Disabilities

by William J. Vaugh (February 1985)

John was identified as learning disabled in third grade. At 18, he dropped out of school. He is now unemployed and totally dependent on his family for financial support.

Recently, John began attending adult education classes to obtain a high school equivalency diploma; but he found these courses extremely frustrating because of his fifth-grade reading level and the mismatch between the teacher's instructional format and his own learning style. The specter of failure that haunted him for more than a decade of schooling looms again. He feels angry and bewildered. He has come to an educational dead end.

Until recently, there was little that anyone could do to help John and others like him, since most special education programs that were developed in response to P.L. 94-142 require that students be enrolled in public or private school. Usually these programs end when a student graduates or leaves school. If such students wish to continue their education at a later date, they are legally adults and literally on their own.

Now, Fairfield County, Connecticut, offers a program designed to provide services for learning-disabled adults. Known as Project ABLE (Alternatives for a Better Learning Experience), the program is geared specifically to individuals, age 16 and older, who have left school and have either been classified as learning disabled or who have experienced a great deal of difficulty with academic subjects.

The program was the brainchild of Patricia Calise-Giannini, a special education teacher in Norwalk, who serves as its director. She and her partner, Sally Hutton, also a special education teacher, make up the teaching staff of Project ABLE. Calise-Giannini began by discussing her idea with the director of adult education for Norwalk, who supported the idea wholeheartedly. She also received the support of the Connecticut Association for

---

William J. Vaugh is assistant principal at West Rocks Middle School, Norwalk, Conn.

49

Children with Learning Disabilities (CACLD). After drafting a proposal that detailed the philosophy, goals, format, and financial needs of the program, she presented the idea to the Norwalk Board of Education, which approved the program in June 1982 and encouraged her to implement it the following semester.

Project ABLE is housed at Norwalk High School, where the regular adult education program also is located. Project ABLE is open at no cost to all eligible students in the Fairfield County area.

Students learn about Project ABLE from newspaper accounts, referrals from guidance counselors, or word of mouth. The records of those students who have previously been diagnosed as learning disabled are sent to Project ABLE (with the students' written consent). Those who have not been tested previously take the Woodcock-Johnson Psycho-Educational Battery so that the staff can pinpoint their disabilities.

All students take tests in mathematics and reading to assess their current abilities, and the staff sets up an individualized program for each student that is geared to that student's background and goals. Students meet twice each week in the evening for 10 weeks a semester, studying either language arts or mathematics. The emphasis in Project ABLE is on sequentially structured remedial lessons, and students also are encouraged to learn through a variety of modalities. For example, they may use tapes, calculators, or computers as aids. It is even possible for some students to bring friends to class to help them with their notetaking.

Project ABLE makes learning as functional as possible. Since the lessons are individualized, many students work on problems or improve skills that are directly related to their jobs. At the same time, large-group sessions in which students share experiences related to their learning disabilities are an integral part of the program; these meetings help develop group spirit and motivate students to achieve.

During its first year of operation, 40 adults — ranging in age from 17 to 53 — completed one or both semesters in Project ABLE; and not one dropped out in the middle of a semester. Posttests revealed that increases in mathematics scores ranged from 1.6 to 4.0 grade levels. Increases in language arts scores ranged from 0.6 to 2.0 grade levels. Moreover, students say that they are "comfortable" in the classes, that the teachers "know how to teach" them, and that they no longer feel "alone" with their learning problems.

Although still in its infancy, Project ABLE already fills a gap in the educational system of Fairfield County. As Beryl Kaufman, executive director of CACLD, put it, "Learning disabilities are not problems that children outgrow."

Update — *Mr. Vaugh writes that students who have gone through Project ABLE, which is now six years old, have met with a great deal of success. Obviously, the program fills a void in the education of learning disabled adults.*

Altogether, 120 students have finished the program. They ranged in age from 17 to 59, but most were in the 20-25 age bracket. All but two are currently employed in such diverse areas as filing clerk, teacher's aide, food service employee, landscaping helper, computer operator, graphic artist, nurse, assembly worker, security guard, or business maintenance and construction.

Three students have applied for and passed the state license test in hairdressing and journeyman electrician. Twenty went on to higher education in such institutions as Norwalk Community College, American International College, Manhattanville College, Housatonic Community College, Southern Connecticut State University, Porter-Chester Institute, and the New York Restaurant School. These students are pursuing careers in nursing, teaching, drafting, auto mechanics, restaurant management, carpentry, etc.

One student graduated from Manhattanville College with an M.A. in special education and is currently teaching a special education class.

Staff Development with a Difference

Houston Program Trains Effective Substitutes

by **Ronald G. McIntire and Larry W. Hughes** (June 1982)

The value of a cadre of effective substitute teachers cannot be overstated. The average student spends seven days out of every school year with a substitute teacher. That comes to 84 days (nearly half a school year) during 12 years of schooling.

Moreover, the number of good substitute teachers is likely to decline just as the need for them increases. The teacher shortage that many forecasters are predicting will make full-time positions available to many of the most experienced and most effective substitutes. At the same time, teacher contracts today include more sick leave and more time off for personal matters and professional development than ever before. Thus the number of days to be filled by substitutes is likely to increase, and the shortage of capable substitutes threatens to become acute.

But it doesn't have to be so. We at the University of Houston, in cooperation with Texas Southern University and the Houston Independent School District, have developed 20 two-hour inservice training classes that specifically address the special demands that face substitute teachers. We call these classes Substitute Teacher Education Modules (STEMs). Substitute teachers who complete 12 STEMs (24 hours of instruction) and pass a qualifying examination are eligible to receive an additional $5 per workday for the following three years.

We invited 10 substitute teachers to help us develop a list of essential skills for substitute teaching. We then sent this list to other substitute teachers, to full-time classroom teachers, and to building principals, so that they could verify the importance of each skill. From this validated list we carefully constructed the training modules, each with a single focus.

Ronald G. McIntire is an associate dean in the College of Education at the University of Houston, where Larry W. Hughes is a professor of educational leadership and cultural studies. Readers who wish to learn more about STEMs may write to Mira Baptiste, Staff Development, Houston Independent School District, 3830 Richmond, Houston, TX 77027.

We discovered early in the planning of STEMs that many of the skills of substitute teaching are different from those that regular teachers employ. For example, substitutes know little or nothing about the students with whom they will be working. Variety typifies their teaching assignments. One substitute teacher told us, "I was trained to teach students who were already seated. As a substitute, I first need to know how to get them to sit down!"

This and other problems of classroom management receive special emphasis in the STEMs program. Participants learn to use behavior modification and other disciplinary techniques; they also study principles of learning that help to promote productive classroom behavior. For example, substitutes learn to use positive reinforcement to encourage behaviors that they approve and to ignore minor distractions that do not significantly disrupt the class. The module on motivation teaches substitutes how to help students succeed, which in turn improves classroom behavior. Participants learn to set tasks at appropriate levels of difficulty, to supply prompts when needed, and to divide long assignments into many shorter, more readily accomplished tasks.

Other STEMs emphasize such practical matters as communication skills, the mechanics of filling out school forms, understanding school district policies and state and federal laws, and the use of textbooks and materials adopted by the state. Perhaps the most practical module deals with planning an effective lesson on short notice.

The STEMs are taught by university professors, classroom teachers, or experienced substitute teachers. At the start of each module, each participant receives a small handbook containing the STEMs objectives, a transcript of class materials, and sample examination questions and answers. These materials help participants prepare for the qualifying examination that tests their mastery of the techniques covered by the module.

We do not claim that the STEMs program is a panacea, but the program offers training and recognition to substitute teachers. It also affords greater peace of mind to administrators who must sometimes staff their classrooms on very short notice.

Update — *Ms. Baptiste writes that the STEMs program has stood the test of time. One change was made in 1987, however, due to financial constraints. Instead of the $5 extra per workday for substitute teachers who complete 12 STEMs and pass the qualifying exams, substitutes are being paid the regular rate to participate in 30 days of training.*

The program is being tested in other districts. Baptiste received approximately 150 requests for additional information after the Kappan *article appeared, and 40 sets of the training materials used in the Houston district ($30 per set) have been sold.*

A School District and a University Join Forces to Train Administrators

by **Ray Cross and Terry Littleton** (September 1986)

Two years ago, planners in the Corpus Christi (Texas) Independent School District realized the difficulty they faced in implementing an inservice training program for building-level administrators. Because faculty members at Corpus Christi State University had helped the district design its new system for evaluating administrators and because the need for inservice training was identified through the evaluation program, district planners once again decided to use the university as a resource for developing an inservice training program for administrators.

With the endorsement of top administrators at both institutions, plans were developed for a permanent relationship, in which the university conducts annual seminars to meet the inservice training needs of the school district's field administrators. Both the evaluation system and the training program for administrators were developed with the advice and consent of a steering committee composed of building-level administrators, thereby ensuring the support of those most affected by the new system.

The district first used its new evaluation system during the 1983-84 school year. Employing established criteria and procedures, central office administrators evaluated principals, and principals evaluated their administrative subordinates. During the final evaluation conference of the year, the evaluator identified the areas in which each administrator most needed to improve. Because it was not possible to design a unique inservice training program for each administrator, a method was devised for grouping administrators with similar needs. This responsibility fell to the steering committee, with advice from central office administrators and a representative from the university.

Ray Cross is a professor of education at Corpus Christi (Texas) State University, and Terry Littleton is assistant superintendent for instruction, Cotati-Rohnert Park (Calif.) Unified School District.

Each building-level administrator's inservice training priorities were listed on a card that was given to the steering committee. The committee then sorted the cards into stacks of similar training goals. The result was eight inservice training groups addressing the following topics: the use of computers, observation and evaluation of teachers, instructional management, human relations, student management, building-level budgeting and finance, the scheduling and staffing of secondary schools, and the development of middle school programs.

It then became the task of the College of Education to locate an instructor appropriate for each of the eight groups. Because of the small size of the college, faculty planners had to look beyond the members of their own department for staff for the project. Ultimately, six groups were staffed by permanent university faculty, one by a retired superintendent with a statewide reputation for expertise in school finance, and one by a nationally recognized professor from another university.

Planners decided early that the inservice training groups would be operated as seminars, with the faculty serving as leaders. The seminars were to extend over the full academic year on a schedule determined by the participants and the group leaders. Since the seminars were a part of the district's staff development program, the planners decided to conduct the programs during school hours. Flexibility, control by participants, and a practical orientation toward action were to be the hallmarks of the project.

The kick-off for the inservice training program was in June 1984 at the district's annual end-of-school retreat for building administrators. At this meeting, seminar leaders met the members of their inservice training groups and began planning activities for the following school year. The purpose of this early meeting was to acquaint the leaders with the specific needs of group members, so that they could do some general planning over the summer. The seminar activities began early in the 1984-85 school year.

The program has remained true to its intention. For example, the group focusing on program development for the middle school has reviewed the literature on middle school programs and visited a number of middle schools with good reputations. The district has asked this group to recommend directions the district might take in establishing a different configuration of grade-level groupings.

The group focusing on human relations completed a sequence of activities on teacher evaluations. Participants evaluated teachers' presentations on videotapes and took part in role-playing exercises with the same teachers they had just observed. These exercises also were videotaped for analysis by participants, the seminar leader, and a professor of communication.

The group focusing on the use of computers reviewed a variety of uses for computers in schools, including record keeping, scheduling, and teaching. The group now communicates with those central office administrators who are responsible for computer use in the district. The exchange of information between this group and the district office has proved especially useful in helping the central office to understand the needs of computer users.

The costs of the inservice training project are underwritten directly by the two participating institutions and indirectly by the state. The school district provides funds for travel and for the use of consultants who are not members of the university faculty. In turn, the university offers tuition scholarships to the participants and has established a fund to purchase printed materials and computer software to be housed in a principals' center at the university. Since participants are technically enrolled in courses for which the university receives funding, the state is an indirect financial contributor. Permanent faculty members serving as seminar leaders are relieved of one course during the fall semester.

While no systematic evaluation of the project has been conducted, informal evaluations from the participants give the project high marks. One principal's comment was typical: "It seems strange that the university and school district have been sitting side by side for years and never got together." One of the seminar leaders, a university professor, remarked, "I hope that the principals are learning something from me, because I'm learning a lot from them about what is going on in the field right now."

Update — *Mr. Cross writes that the project he described in this article fell victim to a Texas "school reform" bill that handed control of administrator inservice training to the State Education Agency. The state-mandated training required so much time that it was not feasible for the Corpus Christi school district and the university to continue their previous arrangements. Interestingly enough, after two years of prescribed administrator inservice training, the state appears to be moving toward the model described in this article, a vindication of the diagnostic, individualized program developed at Corpus Christi.*

Do It First, Then Talk About It: A Principalship Practicum

by Leonard O. Pellicer, Kenneth R. Stevenson, and Thomas A. Surratt (February 1984)

Preparation programs for school administrators have traditionally emphasized theory over practice. The unhappy result has been that new principals can talk about leadership concepts and management processes, but they may not be able to practice what they preach.

At the University of South Carolina we have long lamented the lack of field experiences in the preparation of principals. Now Richland County School District One in Columbia, South Carolina, has joined the university in developing a cooperative internship program for would-be administrators. The practicum is designed to allow students to 1) observe the functions of a principal; 2) assume leadership in planning, implementing, and evaluating selected practicum experiences; 3) put theoretical knowledge to work; and 4) acquire new knowledge and skills in school administration.

The first step in designing the practicum is for each student to complete a self-assessment that measures his or her knowledge and experience in the major tasks of a principal. The eight major task areas, as we see them, are: 1) instruction and curriculum development, 2) pupil personnel, 3) school/community relations, 4) staff, 5) physical plant, 6) school auxiliary services, 7) organization and structure, and 8) finance and business management.

The student, the university instructor in charge of the practicum, and the site supervisor use the results of this self-assessment to tailor an individualized program that focuses on the areas in which each student is weak. A written proposal outlines goals for the practicum and tentative activities

---

Leonard O. Pellicer is an associate professor of educational leadership and policies in the College of Education at the University of South Carolina, Columbia, where Kenneth R. Stevenson is an assistant professor and Thomas A. Surratt is assistant dean.

that the student is to complete. All written goals and objectives must be specific enough to measure.

Each student selects two major areas of concentration from the eight task areas. One task area receives primary emphasis, and the student is expected to devote a minimum of 40 hours to this area. The other area receives secondary emphasis, and the student must spend a minimum of 10 hours working in this area.

For the major area of concentration, students are required to develop a product or refine a process currently in use at the school site. For example, a student might improve the system of registering students for courses (a process) or develop a new guidebook for parent volunteers (a product). This requirement teaches students to assess a real situation accurately and to take steps to change it. All products developed by practicum students are left at the field site at the conclusion of the practicum. In most instances, these innovations have been adopted by the participating schools.

In addition to activities in the areas of their major and minor concentrations, students must also complete a set of "core activities." These activities cut across all the major task areas and are designed to ensure breadth in the practicum experience. Core activities include such tasks as conducting an emergency fire drill, visiting the home of a problem student, and addressing a faculty meeting. Each student must complete a minimum of 20 core activities.

The practicum takes place over a 15-week semester; summer school students complete the practicum in only 12 weeks. Students who have difficulty completing all requirements in the space of a single semester are granted an additional semester to finish.

During the practicum, the site supervisor provides supervision in the school, while the university instructor periodically meets with students in a classroom setting and visits each practicum site at least twice. During these visits, the site supervisor and the university instructor confer on the student's progress and make any necessary modifications in the practicum activities.

When the practicum is over, each student submits a log book of daily activities and a copy of the product or process developed for the school site. The student and the university instructor review the log book together.

The site supervisor evaluates the student's performance at the practicum site. This evaluation is then mailed to the university instructor. The grade for the course is determined by combining the evaluations of the site supervisor and the university instructor.

At the end of the semester, the students meet as a group to complete course evaluations and to share their practicum experiences with one another. They also complete the same self-assessment that they filled out at the beginning of the semester. After the practicum, students feel far more secure and confident in their abilities as principals. Indeed, many have spent far more than the required 60 hours on practicum activities. Most of them spent this extra time voluntarily, because they enjoyed the chance to grow professionally and welcomed the opportunity to put theory into practice.

Update – *Mr. Pellicer writes:*

There have been no substantive changes in the practicum we described four years ago. We continue to build our principalship training program around the task areas of the practicum experience. Currently, we are developing a pre-assessment exercise for new master's-level students. It involves computer simulations that are closely tied to the major task areas. Cognitive knowledge and process skills of the principalship will be assessed. We hope to increase time devoted to the practicum from three to six or nine semester hours in order to focus more attention on individual needs.

The Kappan *article brought many inquiries; we sent practicum materials to more than 20 states. The State Department of South Carolina has modeled its internship for prospective principals on our practicum, and the University of the Philippines has adopted the practicum for use with their school administration students.*

Countywide Inservice Training Day

by Vicky Ramakka and Robert Huddleston (May 1986)

What do you get when 1,500 teachers, administrators, and teacher aides from four school districts and a community college join one another on the college campus for a day of inservice training? You get 1,500 educators learning together and growing excited about participating in a combined inservice training project.

Each October for the past three years, San Juan College in Farmington, New Mexico, has hosted just such an inservice training day for school districts in San Juan County. By combining their resources, the college and the school districts can offer teachers a selection of more than 90 workshops at minimal cost.

Located in the northwest corner of New Mexico, San Juan College serves an area of 5,476 square miles. Some participants travel more than 80 miles to attend the countywide inservice training day. Many come from schools located on the Navajo reservation, which makes up nearly half of San Juan County.

The inservice training day takes nearly a year to organize. The planning committee includes the associate dean for occupational programs from San Juan College and an assistant superintendent or other high-level administrator from each of the four participating school districts.

All members of the planning committee contribute ideas for topics to be covered in the workshop. Teachers and college faculty members are surveyed for suggestions. School principals and parent advisory committees also are invited to recommend topics. Talented presenters in each district are identified, and the committee also may bring in speakers from outside the area.

At the time this article was written in 1986, Vicky Ramakka was coordinator of community services at San Juan College, Farmington, N.M. Ms. Ramakka is now coordinator of developmental projects for San Juan College. Robert Huddleston was dean of instruction at Maricopa Technical Community College, Phoenix, Ariz. Mr. Huddleston is now dean of instruction, Gateway Community College, Phoenix, Ariz.

By early September every teacher in the four districts receives a list of workshops and is asked to mark first, second, and third choices. Each workshop is coded for grade level (K-14), and the planning committee tries to achieve a good balance of topics. Some workshops, such as stress management or public relations, are useful for teachers at any level, while others are designed for such specialists as librarians or music teachers.

The complex task of matching so many teachers' choices to available workshop spaces is handled by a computer program. If a first-choice workshop is full, the computer assigns the person's second or third choice. Once the matching has been completed, a few workshops are dropped because of lack of interest. However, a great deal of interest in certain topics may necessitate conducting concurrent sections of the same program. For example, workshops covering computers, first aid, and cardiopulmonary resuscitation usually require multiple sections.

Luckily, the number of participants in each workshop varies greatly, so that rooms of all sizes throughout the college can be used. In fact, finding enough space for such a large number of sessions is difficult even for a college with 257,000 square feet of space and a full-time equivalent enrollment of 1,300 students. Classrooms, meeting rooms, every nook and cranny — even the board room — are used.

In every hallway, college personnel are on hand to help visitors find their classrooms. A command center is set up to handle problems and last-minute changes. Even medical services are available should an emergency arise during the inservice training day.

Hosts and hostesses help keep the day's busy schedule running smoothly. They are mostly central administrators and principals of schools in the four districts. Such a system ensures the active participation of these administrators, and many ask to be assigned to a specific presenter so that they, too, can learn more about a certain specialty. The hosts and hostesses meet the presenters when they arrive in town, provide transportation, introduce the presenters to the participants, and help with any equipment.

An especially important part of the job of hosts and hostesses is the handling of evaluation forms, which also serve as attendance records. After reviewing the evaluations from the 1984 inservice training program, William Childress, director of elementary education for the Farmington School District, reported that "we felt very, very good." San Juan County teachers gave the program an average rating of 9 on a scale of 1 to 10, with 10 being excellent.

Each school district, as well as the college, pays a portion of the costs based on the number of personnel who plan to attend. Using each participating district's training budget as a guide, the committee establishes a budget for the event. In addition, textbook and school supply companies are invited to rent display areas in the gymnasium for $60 each. Knowing that they will have the opportunity to contact more than 1,000 teachers, many companies participate; this income helps offset a large portion of the costs.

The net cost to the districts and college for the 1984 inservice training program was approximately $4 per person. This was calculated after reducing the total cost by $2,580 collected in rental fees from 43 exhibitors and by $1,600 contributed by a local bank that paid the expenses of one West Coast consultant, who spoke to bank employees for half a day and also conducted an inservice training workshop. According to Childress, the total cost of a little more than $6,000 to all four districts and the college was less than the amount the Farmington district alone had spent for one day of inservice training in the year prior to the first countywide inservice training day.

Childress believes that, in addition to being cost-effective, the joint inservice training program provides a great opportunity for sharing ideas among district teachers. He calls the cooperation between the college and the school districts a good exchange for both. The college provides the facilities, and the teachers' experience with the college is a pleasant one. Having almost every teacher in the county on campus should also improve the recruiting efforts of the college, since teachers will have the firsthand knowledge to answer many of the questions their students may have about the college.

Another member of the planning committee, Bettie Taylor, curriculum coordinator for the Aztec School District (with approximately 140 teachers and 2,500 students), cites the camaraderie developed among the sponsors as a major benefit. She feels that educators in remote sections of the county are somewhat isolated. Taylor estimates the workload for planning the countywide inservice training program to be about equal to planning a day of inservice training for her own district alone. However, sharing the work with the committee "has built strong ties, fostered acquaintances among the county's educators, and increased awareness of each other's needs. Each district has needs and strengths, and this kind of cooperation builds strengths."

Furthermore, Taylor feels that the planning committee gained insights into what teachers throughout San Juan County perceive to be their training needs. For example, she was surprised at the high interest in such coping skills as stress management and time management. On the other hand, many teachers request help on improving teaching skills specific to their subject area or grade levels because keeping up with the latest technology is also a common concern.

Of course, the cooperation required for a program such as the countywide inservice training day did not spring up overnight. Although the program has been in place for only the past three years, the close ties between the community college and the four school districts date back to 1968, when they joined forces to have San Juan College designated as an area vocational school.

The need to coordinate the schedules of all four districts for the area vocational school students led to the formation of a countywide calendar committee. School and college administrators also began to meet regularly, at first to coordinate the area vocational program. Today this group discusses articulation and other issues of mutual concern. It is currently working on implementing a "two plus two" technical preparation program, in which a student will be prepared for a technical specialty during the last two years of high school and then will continue in the same specialty for two more years at the college to earn an associate's degree.

There are several other advantages to this kind of cooperation. One example is the organization of a county curriculum coordinators' association. Because of their participation on the inservice program planning committee, some members saw the value of meeting regularly to exchange information. In addition, the school districts have recently formed a cooperative to pool their special education funds under P.L. 94-142. San Juan College assists the districts by housing the program's coordinator on campus.

Doubtless the groundwork laid by these cooperative efforts, especially the camaraderie and enthusiasm generated by the countywide inservice training program, will continue to foster more interaction, better use of resources, and better articulation between this community college and the four surrounding school districts.

Update – *Ms. Ramakka writes:*
The program is still flourishing and grows in participation each year. It now attracts educators from several other districts, including Bureau of Indian Affairs and parochial schools, who are charged $25 per person.

The four sponsoring districts and San Juan College collectively budgeted $11,000 for the 1987 inservice day. In addition, 48 commercial exhibitors paid $60 each for display booths.

Participants evaluate the sessions and make suggestions, which are faithfully used to revise the following year's program. The net result, according to William Childress, coordinator, is a change in attitude from "Do we have to go to that?" to requests for more time to attend more sessions.

Akron Combines
Foreign Language Camps with
Effective Inservice Training for Teachers

by Marguerite M. Terrill, Sandra Strauber,
and Henry Cone (May 1986)

Inservice training most often evokes tired resignation, not enthusiastic interest, from teachers. The Akron Public Schools have been combating this lack of enthusiasm by combining an inservice training program for foreign language teachers with an existing foreign language camp for students aged 11 to 16. In the first total-immersion Spanish camp for junior high school students, held in 1981, the campers spent a week at Camp Wanake in Beach City, Ohio. The camp staff consisted of master teachers of Spanish, native speakers of Spanish, and high school and college student assistants.

There were several goals for the student campers. The experience was to sharpen their basic language skills, to present a language and its culture in authentic situations, to allow campers to associate with children from different backgrounds, and to improve attitudes about foreign language and culture. The campers participated in customary camp activities, such as arts and crafts, singing, dancing, swimming, canoeing, and hiking. But all these activities were conducted in the foreign language and were based on authentic activities from the foreign culture. Teachers leading the camp had as much fun as the students. They found the camp to be a great opportunity to sharpen their own language skills, to share and try out new classroom materials, and to socialize with their peers and with native speakers in an informal, nonthreatening setting.

For the first three years, the focus of the Spanish camp was strictly on student learning. On the last day of the 1983 and 1984 camp sessions, the staff and students were asked to complete an evaluation of the camping experience. The responses from the teachers were so positive that the Akron Public Schools developed the French and Spanish Inservice Institutes to

Marguerite M. Terrill is foreign language curriculum specialist for the Akron (Ohio) Public Schools. Sandra Strauber is a retired French teacher. Henry Cone is an associate professor of educational administration at the University of Akron.

combine inservice training for teachers with the camping experience for students.

Each year, teachers and supervisors from the Akron Public Schools plan the institutes, and an administrator from a local university approves these plans. Such approval and cooperation make it possible for the participants to earn graduate credit for taking part in an institute. Moreover, the institutes are conducted concurrently with the French and Spanish camps, and this "living laboratory" permits teachers to interact with student campers while both groups improve their knowledge of the foreign language and culture.

The daily camp schedule best illustrates the rich diversity of activities at the weeklong institutes. Between 7:30 and 11:30 a.m. the teachers taking part in an institute follow the students' schedule, joining them for arts and crafts, songs, and dances. At 11:30, the teachers are grouped according to their levels of proficiency, and they practice conversation on current issues in the target culture. Next the teachers join small groups of campers to observe master teachers leading the campers in conversation. Later in the day, the teachers themselves lead the same groups of campers in conversation.

In the afternoon, the teachers work alone, in small groups, or in one large group, attending pedagogical sessions or simply sharing ideas. They also plan the campers' evening activities. In the past, teachers have planned such activities as a flea market with authentic bargaining, a Mardi Gras, an Olympic competition, a fiesta complete with singing and dancing, a ghost hunt, a treasure hunt, and a sing-a-long.

The teachers eat meals with the native speakers to give themselves opportunities to improve their language skills in an informal, relaxed setting. Conversation at mealtimes also helps the teachers stay abreast of current developments in the target culture. The teachers may choose to remain silent and work on listening comprehension, or they may actively question the native speakers on specific topics.

The institutes change the attitudes of many foreign language teachers about foreign language education. Before the camping experience, some of them might have believed that only the best students should learn a second language; afterward, they understand that languages can be taught for practical use to all types of students. The teachers realize that studying a foreign language need not be a formal, impractical, or elitist exercise. These new attitudes carry over into their classrooms, as they incorporate materials and ideas learned at the institute into their lesson plans.

The French and Spanish Foreign Language Institutes demonstrate that effective inservice training need not be a "mission impossible." Working with university faculty members, the master teachers help design and implement inservice training programs in which theory and practice become truly complementary. By helping teachers stay abreast of current developments in their subjects, by giving them the opportunity to improve their professional skills, and by helping them change their attitudes about their subjects and students, the institutes have been a great success for the Akron Public Schools.

When school district officials begin to criticize teachers for their lack of interest in, appreciation of, or attendance at inservice training programs, they should examine the programs being offered. They need only look at the example of the French and Spanish Inservice Institutes to learn how to plan a successful, worthwhile inservice training program that teachers will look forward to attending.

Update — *Ms. Terrill notes that the Akron inservice program continues this year without change. She has received many inquiries by other districts interested in adopting similar programs.*

A Successful Cooperative Plan for Personal and Professional Growth in Lake Washington School District

by Bettie B. Youngs

This article updates a February 1982 Prototype contribution written by Ms. Youngs and James L. Hager, then deputy superintendent of the Lake Washington School District and now superintendent in the Boulder (Colo.) Valley School District. The original article was titled "A Cooperative Plan for Personal and Professional Growth in Lake Washington School District."

The Lake Washington School District in Kirkland, Washington, has accomplished something all good school executives strive for: a successful, comprehensive, and continuous inservice program for all of its employees. While many inservice programs might be charitably described as "ornamental," Lake Washington's goes beyond the rhetoric and puts theory into practice with measurable results.

When Bud Scarr was hired as Lake Washington superintendent in 1977, he faced a multitude of familiar problems: a balky school board, pressure from parents to get rid of "bad teachers," an adversary relationship between the teacher union and the administration, and low morale among most employees. The district needed new energy and a new focus.

Scarr believed that people are motivated by recognition for doing a job well and by active involvement in the decisions that affect them. Consequently, under his leadership, district employees designed a staff development program that has now been operating for more than three years. The program is supported by a district commitment of approximately $500,000 annually.

A far-seeing staff development committee, made up of representatives of all employee groups in the district, set the following criteria: 1) the pro-

---

Bettie B. Youngs was professor of educational administration at San Diego State University when she collaborated on the original Prototype article. She is currently executive director, the Phoenix Curriculum, Institute for Executive Development, La Jolla, Calif.

gram should be a cooperative effort of the district and its employees; 2) it must be related to the identified needs of the staff and students; 3) it must be planned for and regularly scheduled; and 4) it must be of high quality. Using these criteria, the district developed eight different kinds of personal and professional development programs during the first three years. While comprehensive programs are now available for all district personnel, including business, maintenance, food service, and central office employees, the money has been funneled into eight primary areas.

1. *Instructional Theory into Practice (ITIP)*. ITIP includes formal classroom instruction for teachers, demonstrations of good teaching techniques, and actual in-class monitoring of teachers by the ITIP trainers (who are full-time classroom teachers in the district) and/or by administrators. This program, developed by Madeline Hunter, was introduced to demonstrate the elements of good teaching. Eighty teachers were involved in the ITIP program, and more than 95% of the district's teaching staff had participated in at least one 30-hour ITIP program by the end of the 1979-80 school year.

2. *Inservice Training*. All teachers are required to attend inservice training programs. These programs are designed to instruct the staff in areas mandated by law or by the district, including implementing P.L. 94-142 and sex equity in the classroom.

3. *Building-Level Programs*. In addition to districtwide programs, staff development at the building level is nurtured by categorical allocations of $1,500 per year to each of the 26 schools in the district. These funds are for programs selected or designed by the staff of each school.

4. *General Growth*. This aspect of the program uses the expertise of district personnel and outside consultants in meeting the needs and interests of staff and parents. Last year, 1,750 staff members took part in such general growth programs as Planning for Life, Parent Effectiveness Training, and Project TEACH.

5. *School Board Development*. This program is designed to help the school board work in concert with the superintendent and the administration. Each board member has set aside a minimum of four days per year for development purposes. Board members also are encouraged to attend staff development programs.

6. *Administrator Development*. All administrators spend an average of 12 to 14 days in personal or professional development programs each year. These days are in addition to those spent as participants or facilitators in other segments of the staff development program.

7. *Classified Staff Development*. Each supervisor is required to construct a plan of growth for each classified staff employee under his or her super-

vision. Classified staff members then receive training through programs at the local vocational/technical institute, through consultants and specialists brought to the district, or through outside training courses.

8. *Parent Development.* In 1979-80 the district entered into a cooperative project with the Parent/Teacher/Student Association Council to develop, coordinate, and assist in planning programs for parents. This venture gives concrete form to the idea that the schools can do more for the community than just fulfill their primary obligation of educating its children. They can also extend to parents and other community members the opportunity to learn and improve. In 1979-80 more than 1,900 parents participated in training programs.

The Lake Washington staff development program began on a limited scale with primary emphasis on Instructional Theory into Practice training for teachers. Over the years, both the number of programs and the level of participation has been significant. In 1977-78 classroom teachers spent an average of 10.4 days in staff development, administrators averaged 20.5 days, and 373 classified staff members averaged more than four days each. During the 1980-81 school year 923 teachers spent an average of 10.4 days in staff development, administrators averaged 19 days, and 646 classified staff members spent one day per person.

The real measure of a staff development program, of course, is its effect on students. That relationship is extremely difficult to measure; however, we do have evidence that teachers, administrators, school support staff, and other staff members believe that these training programs do help them perform their jobs more effectively. There has been a significant improvement in staff morale and school climate, a reduction of vandalism in the school, and a significant decline in the number of student discipline offenses. Test scores have improved over the years. Public support for schools, as evidenced by the better than 80% approval of district tax levies and bond issues, has also increased.

The motto, "People are the greatest resource of any organization; investing in people is always sound," has paid dividends for students, parents, and school personnel in the Lake Washington School District. Now, years later, the district's programs have continued to achieve success; and they should continue to do so.

Somebody Does It Right: Field Experience for Preservice Administrators

by Dennis C. Zuelke (December 1983)

It is common knowledge in the education profession that prospective school administrators do not receive enough preservice training. This is so primarily because there are not enough paid internships to go around, and unpaid internships do not attract prospective administrators. Thus degree programs in educational administration often involve only academic coursework, with no supervised practical experiences.

Northeastern Illinois University, as a member of a consortium of three universities in the Chicago area, has implemented an unusual plan to remedy this situation. The university provides future administrators with training while they keep their present positions. The program, called the "administration practicum," is a required component of the master's degree program in administration and supervision. Students receive a total of six graduate credits for the two consecutive semesters of the practicum.

A supervising administrator in the field and a student agree on a few objectives for the practicum; these objectives then become the basis of a contract that specifies the tasks the student will complete during the two semesters. Because both the administrator and the student are usually from the same school or district, it is easier for them to choose from an array of more than 100 tasks those that the student can accomplish without shirking his or her responsibilities (usually teaching).

The tasks fall into the following functional categories: school organization, program, and policy making; administration of instruction and per-

At the time this article was written in 1983, Dennis C. Zuelke was associate professor of educational administration at the University of North Dakota, Grand Forks. He worked with the program described in this article in 1979 and 1980. Mr. Zuelke, now director of the Office of Professional Experiences, University of Wisconsin, Superior, acknowledges the assistance of Marvin Willerman, professor of educational foundations, Northeastern Illinois University, Chicago, in the preparation of this article.

sonnel; school managerial, business, and clerical tasks; community relations; and pupil personnel activities and services. Tasks from at least three of these categories must be included in a student's contract for each semester. Specific tasks from the managerial category might include, for example, reviewing and supervising the custodians' schedule or conducting a faculty meeting. In addition, each student completes a school climate study during the second semester of the practicum.

Practicum students are expected to devote about 100 hours per semester (that is, seven hours per week) to practicum activities. However, most students put in more than the minimum number of hours in fulfilling their contracts. The 200-plus hours that students spend over the two semesters in this field experience more than meet the Illinois requirement for administrative certification.

Each student's university supervisor approves the contract initially developed by the field administrator and the student. Where appropriate, the university supervisor may also suggest changes in the contract; but all three parties must agree on its final form. When the contract has been signed by the student, the field administrator, and the university supervisor, the student is ready to begin the agreed-upon tasks.

The university supervisor meets several times each semester in a seminar with as many as 10 practicum students. These seminars enable students to share experiences, express their concerns, and ask questions of one another and of the university supervisor.

Students also are asked to maintain a log of their practicum activities and of the amount of time that they devote to them. The university supervisor reads these logs and uses them as guides for the summative evaluations of the students. Each student also makes a formal presentation to the seminar on one especially demanding or rewarding task he or she completed during the practicum. In this presentation, the student is expected to show an understanding of the theory and research that inform the particular task. Keeping the log and carrying out the activities related to the seminar all take additional time beyond the 100 hours per semester that students spend at the practicum sites.

A university supervisor also visits each student's practicum site at least twice each semester. During these visits, the university supervisor discusses the student's progress with the field administrator. Often these discussions lead (if the field administrator agrees) to increases in the responsibilities given to the practicum student. Some field administrators even agree to turn over the reins of the school or office to the student for a day or more. During that time, the field administrator often fills in for the student, teaching classes, supervising student activities, and so on.

After two consecutive semesters and more than 200 hours of on-site supervisory experience, Northeastern's educational administration students are well prepared to take on principalships or other supervisory positions. Their experience with a wide range of administrative activities in a school or central office setting gives them insight and understanding, as well as the actual skills that they will need to begin their administrative careers successfully.

Update — *Mr. Zuelke and Mr. Willerman write that there have been no substantive changes that require updating this article. The program continues essentially as described here.*

Tailoring Inservice Training in Science to Elementary Teachers' Needs

by Lowell J. Bethel

This is an update of Mr. Bethel's original Kappan article, published in Prototypes in February 1982.

Historically, science has been given short shrift in the elementary school curriculum. My research suggests that elementary teachers are willing to change this situation, but they need excellent inservice programs to help them do so. The schools in central Texas are combating this problem through a National Science Foundation grant intended to instruct classroom teachers in environmental science.

A study conducted in 1979 convinced me that elementary teachers both want and need further science instruction. Forty elementary schools were selected at random for the study. Data came from 338 day-long classrooms and from a science needs assessment of 254 randomly chosen teachers.

My findings were startling. Elementary school teachers in my sample spent an average of only 2% of each school day (approximately eight minutes) on science instruction. In nearly 60% of the classrooms in my study, no science was taught at all.

The teachers' responses to the needs assessment revealed that a majority of the teachers (68%) felt inadequate when it came to teaching science. Nearly all the teachers (91%) indicated that their backgrounds in science and their experiences in teaching science were too sketchy to have prepared them to present most science concepts to their pupils. However, 73% of the teachers wished to learn more science if a convenient opportunity arose.

Ultimately, undergraduate science training for preservice elementary teachers must improve. In the meantime, however, inservice training must

At the time the original article was written in 1982, Lowell J. Bethel was an associate professor of curriculum and instruction in the Science Education Center, University of Texas, Austin. Mr. Bethel now is assistant dean and director of field experiences, University of Texas, Austin.

take up the slack. Thus, with the aid of a $36,000 grant from the Pre-College Teacher Development in Science Program of the National Science Foundation (NSF), the Science Education Center in the College of Education at the University of Texas developed an inservice training program in science for elementary teachers that offered graduate credit to participants. The grant paid for tuition, other fees, and books. A total of 78 teachers applied for the 48 available slots in the year-long environmental science program.

The environmental focus of the program grew out of topics that the teachers had suggested in the needs assessment, which included weather, rocks and minerals, energy, pollution, conservation, ecology, and plant and animal populations. As part of the program, teachers went on field trips; university scientists also conducted seminars on special topics. During the academic year, all participants planned and conducted two inservice workshops for teachers in the schools within their own districts. Among them, the participants provided a total of 30 inservice workshops attended by 418 teachers.

Tests showed that participants' knowledge of science was greater at the completion of the program than at the beginning. A follow-up survey of participants revealed that, after the program, they spent an average of 100 minutes per school week teaching science.

The initial success of this trial program prompted the development of a comprehensive science inservice program designed to train 165 elementary teachers. Again a needs survey suggested that a major need was greater knowledge of the environment and methods for instructing students in science. A second grant proposal was prepared and sent to the National Science Foundation and the Department of Education. Funding was requested for support of an expanded model program in environmental science for elementary school teachers (grades 4-6). The project was granted funding for a three-year period. The grant also provided funding for 165 elementary school teachers for graduate study up to one year.

Teachers were recruited in triads (each triad including a teacher from grades 4, 5, and 6). This enabled teachers to work together in developing and presenting inservice workshops for teachers within their schools and school systems. The purpose was to maximize cost effectiveness by training teachers to train other elementary teachers. It also was designed to maximize implementation of an environmental science program in the central Texas region.

Because of government and NSF spending cuts, only the first year of the proposed three-year environmental science program was funded. This announcement was made several months into the first year of the program.

Recruitment for the remaining two years was suspended until funding was continued. Unfortunately, this never occurred.

Fifty-five teachers were selected for the first year of the proposed three-year program. They attended classes for one academic year. Again teachers attended seminars in environmental science. Such topics as toxic wastes, nuclear power plants, chemical and sound pollution, conservation of energy sources, and cultivation of land for farming purposes were included. Many of the seminars were led by university scientists. A total of six field trips were made around the state. Laboratory activities also were conducted during several of the field trips.

Again participants planned and conducted two inservice workshops. A total of 92 workshops were conducted during the first year of the program. Over 1,380 inservice teachers attended the inservice workshops. This was more than three times the total number of inservice teachers attending during the first environmental science program. Again a follow-up survey revealed that at least 75% of the teachers (41) continued to teach science on a regular basis. Their reported average teaching time for science was 95 minutes per week. This is, again, a very high percentage of increase in time spent teaching science.

This type of model inservice program, because it meets the specific needs of teachers, can be tailored to any content area. In this way, inservice training can help improve the quality of U.S. education.

A School/University Teacher Exchange Revitalizes Both Participants

by Alex Dubil, Mary B. Hill, and Barbara Neuhard (May 1985)

For one semester, from January to May 1983, a special education professor at Bloomsburg (Pennsylvania) State University and a special education teacher from the Bloomsburg Area School District exchanged full-time teaching responsibilities. Prior to the exchange, the professor had taught special education at the university for 10 years, and the teacher had taught educable mentally retarded students in the public schools for 11 years.

The idea for the exchange was conceived by the participants, who then sought support from their respective institutions. The professor reviewed the proposal with her department head and with the dean of the school of education. Meanwhile, the special education teacher met with her building principal and with the superintendent of the school district. Once the proposal had been approved by the university and by administrators in the school district, it came before the board of education of the Bloomsburg Area School District. At that time the decision was made to continue to give the participants in the exchange the salaries and benefits normally provided by their employers.

The advantages of such an exchange are perhaps best described in the participants' own words.

The teacher's observations. At the beginning of the exchange, I had stage fright. The shift from teaching a small group of young children one week to teaching large classes of college students the next proved to be an awesome transition. But I was determined to persevere.

Early in the semester, I had trouble preparing lecture material. I didn't know how much to include, and I tended to overprepare. As the semester progressed, I felt that both my preparation and the pacing of the classes improved.

Alex Dubil is superintendent of the Bloomsburg Area (Pa.) School District. Mary B. Hill is a professor in the Department of Special Education at Bloomsburg State University. Barbara Neuhard is a special education teacher at Bloomsburg Memorial Elementary School.

I received a lot of positive feedback from the students in my classes. I especially enjoyed talking with students who would drop by my office for one reason or another and stay to chat. I tried to make the students see that it takes more than a degree to be a teacher. I tried to convey to them that they must cultivate a genuine love and concern for children if they are to succeed in the classroom.

My most valuable preparation for the exchange was prior observation of the introductory course that I would be teaching. More firsthand experience with the different kinds of exceptionalities covered in the course — but not included in my regular teaching assignment — would have been helpful as well. My only other suggestion for a future exchange would be to do it at the beginning of the school year rather than at the end.

The professor's observations. For me, the greatest benefit of the exchange was the reassurance that I could still deal effectively with a group of children on a daily basis and enjoy it as much as I once had. After 10 years of being a professor, I had many self-doubts about the quality of my teaching skills, classroom management skills, and so on. Once I got back into the classroom, though, I was pleased to find that I fell comfortably into the routine of classroom duties.

I have no doubt that I learned a lot from this exchange. I became acquainted with materials and tests that I hadn't used before. I had never worked in a public school setting — only in institutions — and this new experience presented many challenges in working with parents, colleagues, and the school administration. Working with the parents of my small class of eight students was especially valuable. I felt personally involved in the lives of my students in a way quite unlike the involvement I feel with my college students.

I must admit that I was uncomfortable with my lack of autonomy in the public school classroom. For instance, after I sent a note home to parents about some matter, I happened to leaf through the policy manual, which said that all such communications should be approved by the principal. Luckily, the principal was very understanding about my mistakes.

The exchange also gave me a much-needed break from my job. Everyone can get in a rut, even in the most interesting job. Any new challenge is refreshing, and returning to a familiar job is almost a new experience because you return with an altered perspective.

Going back to the classroom was not always easy. On many days I left school physically and emotionally drained — I'd forgotten how involved classroom teachers can become. Nevertheless, I believe that I brought a lot to the classroom, and the children gave back at least as much. I am looking forward to doing this again, and I encourage others to consider returning to their professional roots.

The idea of teacher exchanges between public schools and universities is still in its infancy, but some generalizations can be made:

• Teacher exchanges can take a variety of forms. Each exchange can be tailored to meet the needs of the participants and their employers.

• Local teacher exchanges are very inexpensive. The participants can retain their own salaries and benefit packages; thus neither the participants nor their administrative units incur any additional expenses.

• Simplicity is an important element in the success of an exchange program. Exchange programs can easily become entangled in procedural matters and bureaucratic red tape. The success of the Bloomsburg exchange is partly due to its simplicity. From the beginning, we limited the number of items open for discussion to a few, including salaries, benefits, certification, and schedules.

• Administrative support is crucial. Without such support, educators will have little inclination to take part in an exchange.

Our experience has taught us that teacher exchanges can revitalize both professors and K-12 teachers. At the same time, an exchange program enhances community relations, serves as a foundation for partnership between the schools and the university, and enables personal and professional friendships to develop across educational levels. What is more, when university professors and public school teachers feel themselves professionally renewed, their students cannot help but benefit.

Update — *Ms. Hill writes that there continues to be much interest throughout the nation in the idea of school/university exchanges. She and the other authors of this article have described their experiences with such an exchange at meetings of the Pennsylvania Association for Supervision and Curriculum Development, the American Association of School Administrators, and a number of smaller groups.*

Something Special for Students

Flea Market Day

by Antonette M. Burks (April 1985)

The tables are strewn with general merchandise; the bakery is full of home-baked goodies; the bank is open for business. It's 1:00 p.m., 90 minutes before school is dismissed, in my fifth-grade classroom at an inner-city elementary school in Indianapolis. It is Flea Market Day.

"It's time to begin," I say. "Make sure you have your Flea Market money tickets out. Joe, will you pass out the find-a-word ditto? Today you can earn 100 tickets for A work, 80 for B work, and 60 for C work." The children quickly take out their money tickets and pencils and wait for the worksheets.

Then I read off the names of children who have earned the right to a "first choice" visit to the Flea Market. These children eagerly gather their money tickets and move to the tables at the back of the room.

The order in which the children are allowed to visit the tables is determined by the number of items each child has donated to the Flea Market. I keep a simple tally sheet listing those who have brought the most items and are therefore entitled to "shop" in the first group.

As a 12-year veteran of the Indianapolis Public Schools, I was looking for a good way to motivate students to work harder. I wanted them to be punctual, to be involved, to behave themselves, and to achieve. What's more, I wanted the parents to take an interest, too. After months of planning and a one-year trial run, Flea Market Day was born.

The Flea Market has an elected board of trustees that sets up ground rules, and I serve as advisor to the board. Members of the board include the class president, vice president, secretary/treasurer, and two nonvoting members. These students help organize the activities of the Flea Market, and they lead the class in making group decisions. A letter to parents early in the

---

Antonette M. Burks is a teacher in the Indianapolis Public Schools. Another version of this article appeared in her book, *A Teacher's Survival Kit* (Indianapolis: Indianapolis Public Schools, 1983).

fall describes the Flea Market and asks them to donate items and baked goods or to volunteer to be vendors on Flea Market Day.

Each child in the class has the opportunity to earn money tickets each week by exhibiting good behavior and steady attendance and by earning grades of C or better. The tickets are small, color-coded squares of construction paper, each stamped with its value. Every Friday afternoon before dismissal, the class looks forward eagerly to payday. Paychecks are simply booklets that contain weekly accounting sheets showing how many tickets a given student has earned. For each grading period, a new sheet is stapled over the old one.

Record keeping is kept to a minimum. I record each child's earnings weekly on a master tally sheet. During the week I discuss individual gains and losses with the students, reinforcing the agreement that has been adopted by a vote of the entire class. The following agreement is prominently displayed in the classroom.

Our Agreement

To gain money tickets:
1. 10 tickets each day for perfect attendance
2. Overall average grade in main subject areas:

A	230	B +	210	B −	190	C	170
A −	220	B	200	C +	180	C −	160
						Below C −	50

3. 30 bonus tickets for good work outside homeroom; 20 for an honorable mention
4. 30 bonus tickets for good work in classroom project, 20 for an honorable mention

To lose money tickets:
1. One ticket for each minute tardy
2. 10 tickets for each book or homework paper left at home
3. 20 tickets for each F on a test
4. 10 tickets for running or talking loudly in halls, restrooms, or classrooms
5. Lose entire week's earnings for fighting, cussing, or cheating

Payday is also a major responsibility for members of the board of trustees. The secretary/treasurer transfers each child's total weekly earnings from the teacher's master tally sheet to a permanent classroom record book and keeps an ongoing account for each class member. The vice president and the nonvoting board members are responsible for counting out the money tickets for each child's paycheck and for maintaining an adequate supply of the tickets. After each child checks to see that he or she has received

83

the proper number of tickets, the president collects and stores the paychecks until the following payday. The children are responsible for keeping their own money tickets.

It's 1:30 p.m. when I ask the first group to return to their desks. The vendors take a deep breath before the next wave of buyers descends on them. As children in the first group examine their purchases or begin work on their ditto sheets, the second group assembles and moves to the back of the room.

Flea Market Day generally takes place on the last Friday afternoon of each month. The members of the board of trustees usually serve as the vendors on Flea Market Day; they and other student volunteers price the items, work behind the tables, and clean up afterward.

Long, narrow tables from the reading center are pushed together at the back of the classroom. They are covered with a profusion of items donated for sale: old books, outdated magazines, discarded toys, games, puzzles, jewelry, clothing, and even used kitchenware and other household items.

Bakery items are displayed on paper-covered countertops near the windows. The bakery is generally the most popular area. Parents, grandparents, even neighbors will send their favorite home-baked cakes, cookies, brownies, and candies or will volunteer to serve as vendors of bakery items. The goodies are individually wrapped and sold separately.

The bank is in the right front corner of the room. It is a brightly painted cardboard refrigerator carton. The secretary/treasurer sits at a desk inside the bank and conducts business through a cut-out window. Children who need to visit the bank wait their turns on chairs lined up to the right of the box.

The bank charges variable rates of interest on loans and pays variable rates on deposits. For example, a child may borrow 10 money tickets, but he or she will have to repay 11 tickets. Both the borrower and the secretary/treasurer sign a loan contract, specifying the amount of the loan, the amount of interest, and the terms of repayment. Occasionally the secretary/treasurer must turn down an applicant for a loan if, after consultation with the other board members and the board's advisor (me), an applicant is determined to be a poor risk. On the other hand, if a child saves 25 money tickets, he or she will earn one ticket in interest. The savings account booklets resemble quarterly bank statements, showing deposits and withdrawals.

It's 2:15 p.m and time to close the Flea Market for another month. "Make all final purchases," I say, "and return to your seats. Mr. President, will you collect all completed fun dittos?"

All unsold merchandise is collected and stored in a cupboard until the following month. The tables are cleared and returned to the reading center. The vice president and the secretary/treasurer collect all the spent money tickets from the vendors, sort them, and file copies of loan contracts. In 10 minutes, the room is back to normal.

The children eagerly gather up their new purchases and line up. Their smiles say that they have had a good afternoon. At 2:30 the bell rings, and the children are dismissed.

Update — *Ms. Burks writes that she now is in the third year of the Flea Market Day project. From the beginning, she says, she could recognize marked improvements in her students' overall behavior and learning patterns, but had no hard data to prove that the project was indeed the success she believed it to be. So in 1987 she embarked on an elaborate assessment program based on assessment inventories used by Indianapolis Public School psychologists and on articles presenting Sloane's, Rieth's, and O'Leary's ideas on token reinforcement programs. She indicates that she hopes to publish her results.*

The Clarkson School:
Talented Students Enter College Early

by **Gary F. Kelly** (October 1985)

As long ago as 1964, Simon's Rock Early College was founded in order to increase the educational options of talented adolescents in an environment that did not neglect their social and emotional development.[1] Since then, this and other programs have demonstrated that some high school students can successfully undertake college-level work.

Yet, even in the face of evidence that one-third of the coursework in the first two years of college has already been taught in many high schools,[2] that high schools find it increasingly difficult to challenge seniors academically,[3] and that partnership programs between high schools and colleges can work,[4] very few other early college options exist in U.S. education.

In 1977 the board of trustees of Clarkson College of Technology (now Clarkson University) in Potsdam, New York, approved a plan to establish a special division for talented high school students called the Clarkson School. This step was motivated primarily by the realization that education in mathematics and science at the secondary level was failing to challenge better students. In the mid-1970s the New York Commissioner of Education also called for better articulation between high schools and colleges. In 1986 and 1987 the governor's office and state legislature took an initiative to call for the establishment of "High Schools of Excellence" in various regions of the state for students with special talents.

In the fall of 1978, the Clarkson School's "Bridging Year Program" opened. It enrolled 21 students who had completed their junior year of high school and who had demonstrated outstanding interest and ability in science, mathematics, and pre-engineering courses. The program was established solely to give talented high school students access to a solid college curriculum in the sciences and engineering. Clarkson was not facing particularly hard times; regular enrollment was rising, and the endowment was growing. As is now true of many institutions, current university enrollment has

---

Gary F. Kelly is headmaster of the Clarkson School and directs the Student Development Center, Clarkson University, Potsdam, N.Y.

been declining somewhat, from 4,107 students in 1983 to 3,774 students in 1987. Conversely, enrollment in the Clarkson School has risen from 24 in 1983 to 51 in 1987.

In retrospect, I can say that the Clarkson School was established rather naively, with little attention given to the special problems and decisions that would inevitably arise. Nevertheless, the college committed money, space, and staff to a program that would bring high school students to the campus for a head start on college courses and campus life.

Academics. Students in the Bridging Year Program take a freshman college curriculum that is consistent with their educational goals. They take classes with regular college students, taught by college professors.

Most of the high schoolers in the program need only one or two courses (often English or social studies) to complete their high school graduation requirements, and nearly all their schools have been willing to accept college-level courses as substitutes. This has allowed the students to graduate with their high school classes. In the few cases in which the home high school has had a senior residency requirement or has refused to cooperate, we have arranged for students to obtain high school diplomas through the state education department.

During its first three years, the program offered one course just for Clarkson School students that combined an emphasis on communication skills with the study of American history and literature. We hired a teacher solely to teach this course. Even though the course carried college credit, the students did not seem to take it as seriously as they did their other courses.

During the 1981-82 academic year, Clarkson School students were integrated into several sections of a newly instituted freshman humanities course that emphasized communication skills, critical thinking, and some key philosophical concepts of Western civilization. They took this course more seriously, and it has been very popular.

The only special class sections now offered solely to Clarkson School students are a single recitation each week in calculus and another in physics. We have arranged for the major professors in the two courses to teach these recitation groups. Since early-entering students often have not taken high school physics or calculus, this enables us to provide them with as much individual help as they need.

A weeklong inter-term experience that combines learning and recreation is offered each January. The students spend this time in Montreal, taking part in scheduled tours and events as well as exploring the city on their own. We see this experience as an integral part of the educational program of the Clarkson School.

Student life. In dealing with younger students, we have considered it imperative to maintain a small-group atmosphere in living arrangements and to maintain somewhat closer supervision than is typical in college dormitories. The students now live in four houses in a residential neighborhood adjacent to the campus and in one wing of a nearby university dormitory. Graduate students or college juniors and seniors serve as live-in house advisors. In addition, one member of the Clarkson School administrative staff lives in one of the houses. The students eat in a nearby college cafeteria, and one evening each week we hold a "family dinner" for all Clarkson School students and staff in a separate dining room.

To provide for a smooth transition to college life, there is a curfew during the first semester. This is liberalized as the year progresses, and by year's end it has ceased altogether. Visitors are prohibited from the houses after midnight, alcoholic beverages are not permitted, and Clarkson School students are not permitted to have automobiles.

Over the 10-year history of the program, we have come to believe that the residential setting is the most critical factor in students' adjustment to college — and thus in the program's success. The students enjoy the family atmosphere of the houses, and the only problem we have encountered has been setting up quiet hours and other conditions conducive to study in such close quarters.

Personal adjustment. Clarkson School students take part in an extensive five-day orientation prior to the beginning of classes. In addition to preparing students for the rigors of college-level work by providing sessions on study skills, the orientation offers structured opportunities, such as an all-day retreat, for getting acquainted and for building a sense of cohesiveness in the group. We circulate a questionnaire to gain information about personal interests, preferences, and habits that helps us match students with compatible roommates.

Since the academic pressure at Clarkson is great, we realized after the first two years of the Bridging Year Program that it was essential to encourage extracurricular involvement. In 1980 we instituted the Self-Development Program. Each student is required to establish goals and to earn self-development units in five general areas: human relationships and responsibility, physical fitness, cultural awareness, professionals in society, and field trips. The program provides for a great deal of flexibility in the ways that these goals can be met, but it has succeeded in involving students in many aspects of campus and community life that they might otherwise have neglected.

Recruiting and college placement. The program has required more active recruiting than we originally envisioned. At first we feared that the high schools would see the Clarkson School as a competitor for their best students. Therefore, we kept our recruiting efforts very low key. Before long, however, it became obvious that the idea of a head start on college for selected students was highly appealing to parents, guidance counselors, and the students themselves.

Our director of admissions has made students aware of the program by attending regional "college fairs" for high school students. We have also found mailings to sophomores who register high scores on the Preliminary Scholastic Aptitude Test (PSAT) to be a useful recruiting strategy. In addition, we have publicized our admissions criteria, which include being in the top 10% of one's high school class, having a score of 650 or higher on the quantitative section of the PSAT, and having demonstrated academic motivation. Most students who apply are well-qualified for the program, though we occasionally admit unique young people who do not quite meet all our criteria. On-campus interviews help us assess each student more accurately, and open-house events held in the fall and spring give high school students a chance to meet our students and to see our facilities.

Now that the program has been operating for 10 years, we receive about 90 applications for 55 openings. We anticipate gradual expansion.

About 50% of our students have elected to go on to other colleges and universities following the Bridging Year Program. They have received full credit for the college courses taken at Clarkson. We encourage all students to keep their educational options open by applying to at least one other institution. However, satisfactory completion of the program guarantees them a place in the sophomore class at Clarkson.

In 1980 and again in 1982, we distributed detailed questionnaires to all current and former students. We found that the Clarkson School graduates were generally achieving higher grade-point averages than their college classmates, regardless of the college they were attending. They felt that their academic and social preparation had been superior to that of their classmates, both in their home high schools and in college. The Clarkson School graduates also have remained in college at a higher rate (96.4%) than typical early admission students. Only eleven of 331 students have left the program — four were expelled for disciplinary reasons, and seven returned to high school because of weak academic preparation.

The Clarkson School is now gaining national recognition for its innovative program. When reports began to appear decrying dangerous weaknesses in science and mathematics at the secondary level, the Clarkson Bridging Year Program was one of the few existing model programs for high achievers.[5] An extensive review of the program by a committee of Clarkson deans and administrators in 1982 led to the decision to strengthen the program's objectives.

High schools have begun to recognize the value of early college-level experience for selected students, and colleges have begun to realize the long-term benefits of creating such programs. The Carnegie Foundation for the Advancement of Teaching has recently cited a number of such projects across the U.S.[6] As the findings of the various national commissions that have studied secondary education are digested, more options of this sort will be springing up. It is essential that these new programs learn from the experience of existing programs and establish living/learning environments that recognize the physical, emotional, and social needs of younger students.

1. Leon Botstein, "Educational Restructuring in Historical Perspective," in Conference Proceedings, *A Case for Educational Restructuring* (Great Barrington, Mass.: Simon's Rock of Bard College, 1981), pp. 47-55.
2. B.F. Blanchard, *A National Survey of Curriculum Articulation Between the College of Liberal Arts and the Secondary School* (Chicago: DePaul University Press, 1971).
3. Gene I. Maeroff, *Don't Blame the Kids* (New York: McGraw-Hill, 1982).
4. Franklin P. Wilbur, "High School-College Partnerships Can Work," *Educational Record* (Spring 1981): 38-44.
5. National Science Foundation and U.S. Department of Education, *Science and Engineering Education in the 1980s and Beyond: A Report to the President* (Washington, D.C.: U.S. Government Printing Office, 1980).
6. Gene I. Maeroff, *School and College: Partnerships in Education* (Lawrenceville, N.J.: Princeton University Press, 1983).

Update — *When invited to update this article, Mr. Kelly chose to rewrite the original. Most of the changes are minor. Mr. Kelly reports that the Clarkson program appears to remain unique on the American educational scene. Many colleges and universities offer opportunities for early admission, but without much structure for students who so easily can flounder because of their younger age.*

Wisconsin College for Kids Stresses Active, Independent Learning

by Ellen Elms Notar and Robin Deutsch (November 1983)

The University of Wisconsin-Madison held its second College for Kids during June and July of 1982. The program is designed to encourage life-long learning and to develop independent learning skills among gifted elementary students. For whatever else gifted children may be, they are not all capable of sustained independent learning — not without encouragement and direction.

Some 250 elementary students representing all 22 school districts in the university's service area took part. They were chosen by their school districts, using one or more indicators of high ability, including above-average scores on standardized reading and mathematics tests, above-average creativity and/or task commitment, and outstanding abilities in the visual or performing arts.

The children spent each weekday morning for three weeks on the university campus. They were organized into small "family" groups, each consisting of between eight and 12 students, a teacher-facilitator, and university professors and staff members. The teacher-facilitators were experienced elementary school teachers who were concurrently enrolled in a graduate seminar that emphasized the same instructional strategies and objectives as the College for Kids.

Following Joseph Renzulli's enrichment triad model,[1] the College for Kids provided contact with "turned-on scholars" who were actively engaged in solving real-life problems. This kind of enrichment is necessary for the

---

At the time of this article was written in 1983, Ellen Elms Notar was director of Continuing Education and Extended Services in the School of Education at the University of Wisconsin-Madison and director of the College for Kids. Notar is now chairperson of the Educational Leadership Program, School of Continuing Studies, Johns Hopkins University. Robin Deutsch was a doctoral candidate in the School of Education at the University of Wisconsin-Madison and associate director of the College for Kids.

cognitive growth and attitudinal development of highly able students, who too often find that enrichment activities turn out to be little more than games and puzzles. Altogether, the students at the College for Kids worked with more than 60 professors, who introduced the children to their research areas and who modeled problem-solving skills.

A second aim of the program was to teach the children about learning — to teach them the conscious use of systematic, sequential thought. Benjamin Bloom's cognitive taxonomy and David Krathwohl's affective taxonomy[2] provided teacher-facilitators with simple structures around which they could develop learning activities that introduced students to systematic thinking. In the small groups, teacher-facilitators led student discussions of problem finding, problem solving, analysis, synthesis, and evaluation. At the same time, the small groups provided welcome support to young children facing a great many new and challenging experiences in a very short time.

During the first week, the students were given an opportunity to look at the university as a whole and at four general spheres of knowledge: biological sciences, physical sciences, social sciences, and the visual and performing arts. This introduction involved a variety of activities. The students listened to a concert of Renaissance music, observed a chemistry demonstration, peered inside a cow's stomach, and visited the nuclear reactor.

During the second week, the children participated in one in-depth workshop of their own choosing from among 50 that were offered; in the third week, they took part in another workshop. The diversity that this arrangement offers is so great that during the second week a student might take part in a pharmacy or microscopy workshop, while during the third week that same student might be learning about electronic music or lasers and holography.

The workshops were designed to incorporate the specific processes of problem finding, problem solving, analysis, synthesis, and evaluation. In the primate laboratory, for example, professors initially showed the children slides of the behavior patterns of monkeys. Then they divided the children into teams to observe and systematically record the behaviors of a troop of Rhesus monkeys. Later, the teams analyzed their data and constructed ethograms. They discussed differences in the behaviors of various age and sex groups within the troop. Then the professors explained the similarity between the social development of young monkeys and human children, in order to demonstrate the relevance of this kind of research. The professors and the students discussed the kinds of research questions that can be asked about the social behavior of monkeys. Finally, the children separated into small groups to research particular questions; one group of students prepared a report that was placed in the Primate Center library.

One workshop group, calling itself the Star Struck Scientists, worked with the problem of water pollution. The children collected water samples from nearby Lake Mendota and brought them to the environmental studies laboratory for analysis. The end product prepared by this group was a bound booklet of drawings, diagrams, prose, photos, puzzles, and poetry, which discussed the causes of and cures for pollution.

Another workshop group focused on learning about and respecting the diversity of humankind through firsthand analysis of human differences. These students rolled tongues, measured toes, examined ears, typed blood, and took fingerprints. They also studied the relationships of gene to chromosome, chromosome to cell, and cell to body, including the role of chromosomal variation in such illnesses as cystic fibrosis, Tay-Sachs disease, and sickle cell anemia — all foci of current research in genetics at the University of Wisconsin-Madison.

Students in the dance workshop analyzed movement in nature, in art, and in machines. They explored the beauty of synchronized movement, as each student became first a complete individual machine and then a part of a more complex group machine. The children assumed the roles of both spectators and participants as they evaluated their creations.

The 250 participants in the College for Kids during the summer of 1982 were given a list of skills and understandings and were asked to check those that they felt had improved because of their participation. Fifty-four percent believed that they had improved in questioning skills, 51% in problem solving, 34% in understanding of themselves, 77% in understanding what people do at a university, and 60% in understanding why people do research. As if to confirm these figures, in 1981 the College for Kids won the National Association of Summer Sessions Award for the most innovative and creative summer program offered by a college or university in the U.S., Canada, or Mexico.

1. Joseph S. Renzulli, *The Enrichment Triad Model: A Guide for Developing Defensible Programs for the Gifted and Talented* (Westfield, Conn.: Creative Learning Press, 1977).

2. Benjamin S. Bloom, *Taxonomy of Educational Objectives: The Classification of Educational Goals, Handbook I: Cognitive Domain* (New York: Longmans, Green, 1956); and David R. Krathwohl, Benjamin S. Bloom, and B.B. Masia, *Taxonomy of Educational Objectives: The Classification of Educational Goals, Handbook II: Affective Domain* (New York, David McKay, 1964).

Update — *Ellen E. Notar writes:*

Yes, the Wisconsin College for Kids is alive and well at Madison, with very few modifications. The fact that it is portable is borne out by its adoption on other University of Wisconsin campuses and at community colleges. It even spawned a program at the Gdansk, Poland, Institutes of Science and Mathematics. When I was in China last year, I was asked to address the topic of special programs for the gifted at Beijing Teachers University and have since received correspondence that indicates a "College for Children" may be initiated in the Peoples Republic of China.

Junior First Grade:
A Year to Get Ready

by Maizie R. Solem (December 1981)

Children come to kindergarten with mental ages that range from 3 to 8. Developmental lags in language, motor, or perceptual skills are not uncommon, even in kindergartners of average or above-average intelligence. Physical, emotional, and behavioral factors hamper the ability of some 5-year-olds to learn. So do such circumstances as family size, family stability, and experiential background. Thus not all kindergartners are ready for first grade when they reach age 6. Some need more time to prepare and to grow if they are to avoid early academic failure and damaged self-concepts.

To serve such children, the Sioux Falls (South Dakota) School District has offered a junior-first-grade program since 1970. The program started with one classroom for 15 students; today it encompasses five classrooms serving a combined enrollment of 75.

Kindergarten teachers identify candidates for these transitional classrooms. Their own observation and judgment play a significant role in the screening process. In addition, children's scores on the Yellow Brick Road Screening Test (administered in the fall to all kindergartners) and on the Metropolitan Readiness Test (administered in May) are taken into account. The kindergarten teachers also complete an informal Pupil Behavior Rating Scale for each child. When specific cases warrant it, school psychologists conduct additional testing.

Children who may benefit from spending a year in a transitional classroom generally exhibit one or more of the following characteristics.

- *Hyperactivity.* The child cannot sit still. He or she lacks organization. The child's desk may be a mess, or it may be compulsively neat. He or she may be over-aggressive or too shy.

At the time this article was written in 1981, Maizie R. Solem was primary curriculum coordinator, Sioux Falls (S.D.) School District 49-5. Since then she has retired.

- *Perceptual/motor deficiencies.* The child has poor coordination; use of pencils, scissors, crayons, and other implements is clumsy and awkward.
- *Daydreaming.* The child is slow to react. He or she fails to tune in.
- *Short attention span.* The child has difficulty concentrating and is easily distracted.
- *Impulsiveness.* The child does things without thinking and regardless of consequences.
- *Memory/thinking disorders.* The child shows inability to recall and makes inappropriate responses.
- *Perseveration.* The child compulsively repeats a word, a phrase, a drawing, a given piece of writing. He or she is unable to change activities readily.
- *Speech/language/hearing disorders.* The child reverses words, phrases, numbers, letters; speaks inarticulately; or fails to comprehend or respond to verbal instructions.
- *Generally poor attitude toward self or school.* The child seldom participates in instructional or social activities.
- *Learning deficits in reading, math, writing, spelling.*

The junior-first-grade program is optional; parents make the final enrollment decision at an informational meeting in May. Since they have been attending conferences with their child's kindergarten teacher throughout the year, they are already aware of their child's progress and prospects.

Transportation to the transitional classrooms is left to the parents. Because this poses a problem for some families, children who might profit from the junior-first-grade program are occasionally unable to participate. Carpools are often formed, however, to overcome this difficulty.

The junior-first-grade instructional program is designed to improve reading and math readiness; to develop oral language; and to increase a child's ability to understand spoken language, to listen, and to follow directions. Activities focus on developing gross-motor and eye/hand coordination. Teachers nurture social and emotional maturity, self-reliance, self-control, and cooperation. Development of a healthy self-concept is an essential component of the program. The curriculum also includes music, art, and physical education. Health, science, and social studies are taught only incidentally, when appropriate situations arise.

Does the transitional program help youngsters to succeed in first grade? To answer this question, we asked first-grade teachers in May 1978 and again in May 1980 about the achievement levels of their students who were former junior-first-grade enrollees. In 1978 we found that 25% of these youngsters ranked in the top quartile of their first-grade classes, 25% ranked in the lowest quartile, and 50% ranked in the second and third quartiles. In 1980, 28% of the former junior-first-grade participants ranked in the top quartile of their first-grade classes, 70% ranked in the second and third quartiles, and 2% ranked in the lowest quartile. All of these youngsters had been deemed "high-risk" students as kindergartners — youngsters likely to experience failure in first grade.

The Sioux Falls junior-first-grade program is funded entirely by the school district and will be expanded if the need arises. Student success and the enthusiastic reception accorded the program by parents, teachers, and building administrators make evident the value of this yearlong program of specialized assistance.

Plato, in *The Republic*, put it well: "Don't you know that in every task the most important thing is the beginning, and especially when you have to deal with anything young and tender?"

Update — *Although Ms. Solem has now retired from her work as primary curriculum coordinator in the Sioux Falls District, she reports that the program described here continues to grow and flourish. Its structure remains basically the same, but now there are 10 classrooms for the junior first-graders, who number approximately 150.*

Surveys of first-grade teachers show that 97% of the children who complete the program reach the top two quartiles in first-grade achievement and 41% reach the top quartile. Not only do teachers and administrators recognize the program's value, but parental support ensures its continuation.

Ms. Solem received several hundred requests for more information after this article appeared. They came from districts throughout the U.S., and there was even one from Hong Kong. She is aware of at least 12 other districts that have adopted the junior-first-grade idea.

Brown Bag Lunch Programs Provide Food for Thought

by **Ann Hassenpflug** (November 1986)

A talk by a refugee from Guatemala, a concert of American folksongs, and a slide presentation by the director of the local humane society have one thing in common: they are among dozens in the brown bag lunch programs presented in recent years at East High School in Madison, Wisconsin. The brown bag lunches, which started in the fall of 1983, expose the 1,500 ninth- through 12th-graders at East High to a wide range of topics and issues not covered in the conventional curriculum.

The presentations take place weekly (usually on Thursdays) during the two 30-minute lunch periods. Students and teachers attend these programs voluntarily; they do not have to sign up in advance. A teacher will sometimes bring an entire class when the topic is relevant to ongoing classroom activities.

The size of the audience at a given presentation varies from a dozen to about 100, depending on the topic. The presentations take place in a lecture hall that seats approximately 150. This hall is located near the cafeteria and away from classrooms, so that the arrival of students with bag lunches or trays from the cafeteria will not disrupt classes in session.

Students and faculty members are notified of coming programs by means of schedules prepared three times a year and posted in classrooms. Teachers receive the schedule for fall programs in early September, for winter programs in early January, and for spring programs in late March. It is easier to plan the programs in three blocks, because speakers or performers are generally more willing to commit themselves to a date in the near future than to a date six to eight months away.

With the exception of two musical peformances, all brown bag lunch programs have been provided at no cost to the school. Presenters come from within the school or from the Madison community. For example, a professor emeritus at the University of Wisconsin presented fascinating trivia about

---

Ann Hassenpflug is an assistant principal at East High School, Madison, Wis.

language and grammar. The East High School social worker showed slides from her recent trip to Australia. A physics teacher and a teacher of English as a second language joined forces to show slides of their visit to Bolivia and Peru. A central office administrator talked about her husband's relative, writer Robert Pirsig, and about his book, *Zen and the Art of Motorcycle Maintenance*. Local students who won awards in regional and national science contests took part in a panel discussion of their projects.

A native of Syria who attends East High School talked about cultural differences between Syria and the U.S. The owner of a local Mexican restaurant talked about women in the restaurant business. Scientists from the Sea Grant Institute at the University of Wisconsin presented current research findings on the trout in Lake Michigan. Local celebrities, including a television news broadcaster, have provided brown bag lunch programs, as have a string quartet and a brass-and-percussion duo.

As assistant principal, I coordinate the brown bag lunch program. I locate possible presenters through items in the local newspaper, contacts at the university and in community agencies, and recommendations from East High students, teachers, and parents. The number of potential presenters has increased, rather than diminished, over time. I contact each prospect by phone or letter and schedule a program date. The arrangements for each three-month block of programs are completed a week or two prior to the appearance of the printed schedule.

Brown bag lunch programs are publicized in other ways besides the posting of schedules. Teachers find colorful posters in their mailboxes each Monday, which they display in their classrooms to remind students of that week's topic. On the day of a brown bag presentation, the program is mentioned in the morning announcements. A newsletter to parents also includes information about coming programs.

The brown bag lunch program at East High School has shown us that students are interested in knowledge for its own sake. The program has also enabled students, teachers, members of the clerical staff, and parents to see one another as learners. No other program at East High provides a similar opportunity for collegiality.

Such an enrichment program would be easy to initiate at other schools, regardless of grade level. Perhaps the most important outcome of a brown bag lunch program is the positive view it gives presenters and participants of the possibilities of public education.

Update − *Ms. Hassenpflug reports one major modification in the brown bag lunch program at East High since this article was written. In order* *to increase attendance, the weekly programs for 1987-88 were scheduled for varying periods of the day rather than at the lunch hour. Attendance rose dramatically, although the program is still voluntary. Also, attendance is now by class, with teachers making reservations shortly after the semester list of programs is distributed. Ms. Hassenpflug states that both teachers and students are better satisfied with this new approach.*

This Schoolwide Project Promotes Academic Learning and Human Understanding

by Matthew King (May 1984)

Everyone agrees that creating a sense of community within a school is a worthwhile goal — but how to do it is another matter. Carlisle Junior High School, in Carlisle, Massachusetts, is the site of a curriculum project that brings together 220 children of different ages to work with each other and a variety of adults on activities related to a single topic. In this way we promote mutual understanding, reinforce academic skills, and impart new knowledge.

The project began with a suggestion for a schoolwide activity that would allow students to cross the boundaries of grade level and subject matter and to focus on a single topic. In September 1981 we formed a seven-member committee of teachers and administrators to begin planning such an activity for the following spring. The committee decided to organize a three-day program during the final days before spring vacation. The topic we chose was "The Forties." We decided to organize the school into three teams, each team including students from grades 6, 7, and 8, as well as teachers and administrators. We also assigned to each of the teams one of three broad subtopics: the war, the home front, and the postwar era.

Next we established a set of goals: students would become familiar with the sequence of events in the Forties; they would establish a personal connection with someone who had lived through the decade; they would explore the connection between such contemporary issues as nuclear energy and human rights and the events of the Forties; and they would gain an understanding of the texture of daily life in the Forties. We also decided to show a movie, "The Best Years of Our Lives," to be followed by small-group discussions. And we decided to end the three days with a record hop, complete with clothing typical of the Forties and an appearance by the high school "swing" band.

Matthew King is superintendent of the Carlisle (Mass.) Public Schools and principal of the Carlisle Junior High School.

By early January we had added several more schoolwide activities to complement the work to be done by the three teams. The five units that we devised, which I describe below, were to be planned by committees composed of representatives from each team. These unit activities would account for two-thirds of the three-day program, with the balance left for each team to plan on its own. A brief outline of these units follows.

1. *Preparation review*. To spark student interest, the project was introduced after the winter recess with a social studies assignment that required each student to collect an oral history from someone who had lived through the Forties. At the same time, language arts teachers encouraged youngsters to read novels set in that decade, and science teachers introduced concepts about nuclear energy. Finally, I sent a letter to parents that explained our project and invited them to participate by discussing the Forties with their children and by re-creating the home environment of that decade — by turning off the television set, for example.

2. *Orientation*. To kick off the three-day program, each student received a folder containing about 20 photographs and documents that related to the Forties. Working in small groups with a teacher, the youngsters analyzed these materials and, over the course of the three days, created collages portraying the decade. Immediately before the record hop, the collages were judged by a panel of students.

3. *Atomic bombing of Japan*. The students watched a documentary film on the decision to drop the atomic bomb. This was followed by small-group discussions, led by teachers, that considered whether and in what sense the decision had been "right."

4. *Home front*. Several teachers presented a slide/tape show on such aspects of the Forties as heroes, cars, and advertisements. Following the 20-minute presentation, small groups sifted through stacks of old *Life* magazines to identify some of the topics covered in the show.

5. *Leaders, followers, victims*. This unit examined the political and social changes that took place in Germany and led to the war and the Holocaust. The events were presented not simply as examples of the unique evil of the Nazis but as powerful reminders of the extremes of human behavior. As part of this unit we introduced the students to the experiment conducted in an American high school in which a teacher re-created a movement similar to the Hitler Youth.*

While we were developing these schoolwide units, we also put together activities for our teams. My team, for example, planned an obstacle course,

---

*Christopher Hyde, *The Wave* (New York: Doubleday, 1979).

modeled on Army basic training; conducted jitterbug lessons to insure that the record hop would be authentic; and researched the plight of Japanese-Americans during the war.

During the three days of the program, not one problem surfaced. Sixth-, seventh-, and eighth-graders worked together smoothly. The students participated enthusiastically and sensitively in activities and discussions that some of us had thought would be too complicated or too emotionally charged.

Our experience with this project demonstrated that we can create opportunities to allow children of different ages to work with one another and with adults in activities that encourage significant academic learning and build better human relations, despite the constraints of an age-graded school. One of our students described the experience as well as I could:

> I enjoyed the three days spent studying the 1940s because they gave me a chance to work with people (students and teachers) that I had never worked with before. Those three days gave me chances to express my ideas on controversial issues where there was no right or wrong answer, . . . to learn what others think of my personal feelings, and to hear their opinions. . . . But best of all, those days gave me a chance to learn many things about the Forties that I had never known before, . . . and they gave me a chance to learn while having fun — something that is not usually possible in a regular school class.

Had we been concerned solely with the academic side of the project — that is, with what students learned about the 1940s — the three days would have been a clear success. But just as important to us was the way the experience enriched our total school life. We became a community of learners, with children and adults learning side by side, seriously considering how events in the past affect contemporary issues. Not surprisingly, we have continued the project in subsequent years; last year our topic was "the Future," and in this Olympic year we are concentrating on "Global Understanding."

Update — *Mr. King writes:*
Re-reading my 1984 article caused me to realize how far we have come since then. What began as an effort of the faculty in grades 6-8 has evolved into a festival for our entire K-8 school. Following the "Forties" project, we indeed did carry out a similar three-day festival titled "The Future." I remember clearly the culminating event of those days in 1984. With the aid of our local Department of Public Works, we buried several garbage cans that had been converted into giant time capsules to be opened in the year

2000. The most interesting development of that festival, however, was the fact that teachers from the elementary grades saw so much going on that looked like fun that they expressed a desire to join in.

As a result, over the next two years we planned and carried out two festivals around the topic, "Global Understanding." This time the entire school of 500 children and 50 adults divided into five teams organized around regions of the world (Europe, Asia, the Middle East, Latin America, and Australia). As we had done with "The Forties" and "The Future," each team developed a comprehensive curriculum for three days, an undertaking that requires considerable time and effort. For example, on the Middle Eastern team we had slide shows by people who had visited various countries. A guest from Iran explained the Islamic religion; we ran a model Passover Seder; we enjoyed regional dancing and foods; and we read stories and created mosaics. Our experience has taught us that these festivals work best when the activities bring children together in active involvement. As we suspected, the greater the age range the easier it is to work with mixed ages. We also learned that these programs breathe life into the notion of the school as a community, a value often expressed but infrequently achieved.

We have been forced to discontinue the festivals for the past two years while our small district completes a large school construction project that reduces the available space. Once the construction is complete, we will have a new auditorium and a facility that will enable us to return to our festivals.

At the same time, our experience with these festivals has helped us to see other opportunities that can be created within schools to bring people together; hence, our school is distinguished by much more collaboration between different grade levels. For example, we are now divided into "community" groups of approximately nine children (grades 1-8) and one adult, who meet monthly to celebrate a seasonal holiday. Before Christmas vacation this year, each group was visited by an elderly citizen who shared his or her experiences in celebrating a holiday, after which the entire school met outside to sing holiday songs. As you can see, we continue in our quest to be a genuine community of learners.

Introducing Talented High School Students to Teacher Education

by **Rose A. Howard and M. Serra Goethals** (March 1985)

Efforts to attract talented young people into teacher education programs have just begun to receive national and state-level attention. In the wake of the excellence movement, support for scholarships, grants-in-aid, and forgivable loans has been growing in a number of states and at a number of institutions.

At Bellarmine College, in Louisville, Kentucky, we designed "Introduction to Teaching," a college course offered for credit to high school students. We had two purposes in designing the course. First, we wished to introduce talented high school students to teacher education. Second, whether they ultimately decide to pursue a career in teaching or not, we wanted the students' attitudes toward teachers and teaching to be based on facts rather than on rumors and unsubstantiated opinions.

Since 1971 Bellarmine College has had an Advanced Credit Program through which the college faculty and principals of participating public and private high schools identify college-level educational experiences that can be completed by high school students, who earn college credit for them. This program seemed like a natural home for our experimental introduction to teacher education.

"Introduction to Teaching" was offered in the fall semester of 1983. The course enrolled 21 high school juniors and seniors, who attended 75-minute sessions, held weekly in the late afternoon on the college campus. The course consisted of three five-week modules. The modules were designed by the directors of elementary, secondary, and special education at the college; and the instruction in each module was presented by its designer.

The sessions covered topics ranging from developmental differences among children to specific curriculum materials for teaching specific skills. Students were assigned weekly readings, and the subsequent discussions proved lively and challenging.

Rose A. Howard is director of secondary education at Bellarmine College, Louisiana, Ky., where M. Serra Goethals is head of the Education Department.

The students were required to attend all sessions, complete all assigned readings and activities, and write a four- to six-page paper. When all requirements had been completed, students were awarded grades; those who received a grade of B or above earned college credit.

Both before and after the course, we gave the students the same 12-item questionnaire and asked them to rate their perceptions of teaching. At the end of the course, 100% of the students said that they viewed teaching as a respectable profession, although 9.5% said that they had little interest in becoming teachers themselves. Before the course began, only about one-third of the students said that parents or others had strongly encouraged them to enter the profession of teaching, but by the end of the semester this figure had risen to slightly more than half of the students. We attribute the increase to changed perceptions of parents' attitudes as the students gained new knowledge of − or perhaps expressed a growing interest in − teaching.

Before the course began, 85% of the students said that some of the people they most admire are teachers, and this figure remained the same at the end of the semester. The percentage of students who said that the requirements for becoming a teacher are demanding increased significantly, however − from 66% before the course began to 85% afterward.

Overall, the responses of these 21 students after they completed the course showed more positive attitudes toward teachers and teaching than did their initial responses. Thus we seem to have achieved part of our aim − dispelling negative attitudes toward teachers and teaching. Whether we have succeeded in attracting any of these talented students to pursue teaching as a career we cannot yet say. But we can say that their ultimate career decisions will be less influenced by the myths that surround teacher education and more solidly grounded in the reality of teaching.

Update − *Ms. Howard and Ms. Goethals recently checked to see how many of the 1983 high school students who took Bellarmine's "Introduction to Teaching" actually completed a teacher preparation program. A gratifying 38% had done so. Subsequent classes show similar results: Between 25% and 50% of these talented high school students have enrolled as prospective teachers.*

Following publication of this article, Ms. Howard and Ms. Goethals had numerous requests for specific information. As a result, programs with a similar emphasis have been developed at St. John's University, Rhode Island College, Louisiana Tech University, Kent State University, the University of California at Los Angeles, and in the Nassau County, New York, school system.

Expanding Horizons:
University Professors Serve as Mentors
for Gifted Middle-Graders

by **Iva Dene McCleary** and **Susan Hines** (May 1983)

How can a school district help a gifted student in the middle grades to study the production of antibodies in the human body — or the mechanisms of photosynthesis? The Department of Special Education at the University of Utah and the Gifted and Talented Project of the Granite (Utah) School District have found the answer: a joint program that gives gifted fifth- and sixth-graders a chance to work with university professors. In addition to meeting these children's special needs, the program provides an occasion for cooperation between the university and the public school system.

The spark for the program was ignited when school district officials approached the senior author with the problem of providing enrichment opportunities for gifted youngsters whose interests outstripped school district resources, facilities, and personnel. She knew of a few university programs for young students, such as the Young People's University Project.* Such university programs for young children are often paid for in part by student fees, which tend to exclude some children.

We decided to try a different approach. We envisioned university professors serving as mentors to gifted fifth- and sixth-graders during the school year. This part of the project was to last two months — allowing the mentors enough time to become acquainted with the students and their special interests. Then the students would come to campus for a day to take a firsthand look at university research and campus life. The extended earlier contact between mentors and students made it easier for the mentors to plan beneficial on-campus experiences for their students.

---

*John Bruscemi, "Young People's University: Challenge, Honor for Gifted Youths," *Phi Delta Kappan* (April 1981): 600.

Iva Dene McCleary is assistant professor and director of community affairs, Department of Special Education, University of Utah, Salt Lake City, where Susan Hines [now Chesteen] is an assistant professor of management in the Graduate School of Business.

We limited the number of students who could take part in the project to 40, partly to keep expenses down and partly because this was a pilot project. We also were unsure whether a large number of university professors would be willing to donate their time.

Teachers and principals in the three schools that participated in the district Gifted and Talented Project identified students and their specific areas of interest. One teacher from each school was selected to coordinate the project at the school level and to attend the on-campus activities. The students who were recommended were those who seemed most likely to benefit from the opportunity to pursue their interests under the guidance of a university professor. A list of these students and their areas of interest was then forwarded to the Department of Special Education.

Recruiting professors to serve as mentors turned out to be very simple. Department heads identified individuals in their fields who might be willing to serve as mentors. We then contacted these faculty members and explained the project to them. Faculty mentors from the fields of biology, chemistry, mathematics, political science, law, English, computer science, physics, and theater agreed to participate in the project.

Next we matched students with mentors, according to the students' interests and the mentors' areas of expertise. The students then wrote letters to their mentors, telling about themselves and their special interests, and a dialogue that was to last two months began between mentors and students.

Between two and eight students were assigned to each mentor; the average group size was four students per mentor. Our evaluation data later indicated that eight students are too many for a single mentor to deal with effectively. Students from these large groups reported that they would have liked to explore individual interests to a greater degree, and mentors of large groups reported that they would have preferred more personal contact with individual students. In the future we plan to hold group size to between three and five students.

All the interaction between mentors and their students during March and April prepared the way for the highlight of the project. The students were brought to the university to spend a day on campus with their mentors. This enabled the students to work with their mentors, to explore campus facilities, and to discuss (or participate in) experiments. All program participants gathered for luncheon and a brief orientation to the university. At that time, speakers explained the admissions requirements of the university and the possibilities for early registration.

Because the interactions between students and mentors varied considerably, we chose to do a post-only evaluation. We sent forms to students, teachers, and university faculty mentors. Eighty-three percent of the students responded (on a five-point Likert scale) to seven questions, as well as to two open-ended ones that gave them opportunities to report elements of the program that were important to them and to recommend changes.

Seventy-five percent or more of the responding students ranked three program elements highest (that is, as 1 or 2 on the five-point scale): 1) the importance of the visit to them, 2) the efforts that their mentors had made to answer their questions, and 3) the things they had learned about opportunities that the university had to offer. Slightly fewer students (70%) ranked as 1 or 2 the new things they had learned about their areas of interest. Our analysis of responses to the open-ended questions indicated that many students felt capable of handling their subject areas in more depth and specificity than they felt that the program afforded. Students rated the orientation to the university as lowest in importance; only 64% of the respondents rated this program element as a 1 or 2.

The students also rated highly the helpfulness of the experience in making career choices and the helpfulness of the experience in choosing an area of study. But these two items were not major objectives of the project.

The open-ended questions asked, "What were the most important things about this program for you personally?" and "What kinds of changes would you recommend if this project were to be repeated?" Student comments about the important things fell into four categories: 1) learning more about their specific areas of interest, 2) learning about the variety of subjects offered by the university, 3) meeting new people and talking to mentors, and 4) learning about careers and college. Students suggested two changes in the program: 1) smaller groups and 2) more advanced discussion in their areas of interest.

Nine of the 10 professors who served as mentors returned the evaluation forms. All but one of them ranked the experience as very worthwhile and found the students adequately prepared. The professor who demurred on these two counts was a substitute mentor who had not had the benefit of two months of contact with the students. This underscores the importance of the early and extended dialogue between students and mentors. Six mentors believed that "this was an activity in which the university should be engaged," one disagreed, and two did not respond. Four of the mentors favored "a time set aside during the summer for a more extended experience." Three disagreed, and two did not respond to this question.

All the coordinating teachers rated the experience as "very beneficial" and "highly motivating" for the students. The teachers perceived the most important benefits of the project to be motivational. For example, some students changed their junior high school programs to include honors classes as a result of this experience. Teachers' suggestions for improvement focused on providing more experiences of this kind and increasing the number of students and mentors participating. Another area of concern to teachers is our expectations of them. In future activities, we plan to offer opportunities during the on-campus experience for teachers to explore such topics as the education of the gifted.

Universities are often accused of not relating to their communities, and colleges of education are often criticized for being unresponsive to the public they serve and to other university departments. Cooperative programs are one means of countering these charges. Such programs can provide valid services to young students and build communication between a university and its public. Moreover, they can foster communication between a college of education and other units of the university. The good news from Utah is that the mentor project — incorporating changes suggested by students, teachers, and mentors — is being repeated this spring.

Update — *Ms. McCleary writes that the gifted and talented student project described here was continued for two years after the article appeared in 1983, but was then the victim of funding cuts for gifted programs. However, she conducted a follow-up evaluation indicating that a project such as this has good long-term effects beyond those anticipated. Many of the gifted middle-graders in the project have gone on to advanced and honors programs in their areas of interest. Several have maintained an informal relationship with their university mentors and a few have participated in summer projects with them. University professors who have continued with the project, both formally and informally, report that they found it both stimulating and surprising.*

Teachers and gifted students in the Granite District continue to report more use of university facilities such as libraries and laboratories. They make more contacts with professors in specialized fields of study. Ms. McCleary also notes that the project resulted in a variety of other cooperative activities involving the district, the Department of Special Education, and the University of Utah. For example, several summer programs designed specifically for gifted elementary and secondary students are offered through the Division of Continuing Education. Concurrent enrollment and special arts and theater projects continue to flourish.

Collecting for Fun, Education, and the Arizona Kidney Foundation

by Emilie Walker (January 1987)

What does a million look like? Adults routinely talk about numbers in the millions and billions, numbers even they can barely conceive. But how does a child come to understand a number so large?

In the fall of 1985, my 32 fourth-graders set out to discover exactly how much one million is — with pull tabs. The project, which ran from just after school began in the fall through February 1986, soon became an enjoyable way to sharpen math and communications skills. It also enabled Glendale (Arizona) American School to show its support for the Arizona Kidney Foundation.

When the class first approached the project of collecting a million things, the students voted to collect popsicle sticks, bottle caps, and pull tabs. Yet once the collections were under way, we discovered that tabs would quickly outnumber sticks and caps. So we narrowed our goal to one million pull tabs.

Initially I called friends, relatives, and colleagues and asked them to join in the project by saving their tabs. Students brought their tabs from home, picked them up after sporting events, and collected them from neighbors, relatives, businesses, and service organizations. Students from other classes contributed tabs; one second-grader regularly brought in a thousand or more. Senior citizens in a neighboring town contributed tabs, and people in other states sent tabs to us.

We also conducted a series of after-school expeditions. A small group of students would accompany me to a grocery store or nearby business to collect tabs. These expeditions took place twice a week, and each student in the class took part in at least one.

We displayed the beginning of our collection (more than 52,000 tabs) on our classroom wall. We arranged groups of 10 tabs into groups of 100 and then into rows of 1,000. For a while, the children counted and strung

Emilie Walker is a fourth-grade teacher at Glendale (Ariz.) American School.

tabs during their free time, but most of the tabulating was done by students and parents at home.

We developed pull-tab math exercises from the project. Every morning we added the students' contributions to arrive at a daily total, and then we added this daily total to our grand total. In our pull-tab math, we easily discovered such weaknesses in the students' math skills as handling zeroes and keeping numbers in their proper columns. When the children began to lose interest in our ever-growing total, we did a countdown, subtracting our total from a million to see how many tabs we still needed to collect.

We also made bar and line graphs, subtracted, estimated, computed averages, and worked story problems. A bar graph under our wall collection showed each student's contribution for the month. A second graph recorded each month's grand total. During the second semester we multiplied and divided with our tabs. How much did 630 cans of pop cost at 40 cents per can? How many six-packs do 126 cans represent? The students were eager to work on such practical problems.

The project also gave students the chance to set goals for themselves and to strive to reach them. Some children would set weekly goals. Others worked to beat Jaime, who consistently collected the most tabs. The school's science specialist also challenged the students: if the class collected 100,000 tabs before Christmas, it would receive a rocket set. After easily meeting this goal, the students set the more difficult goal of reaching 200,000 tabs by November − a goal they did not reach.

The project also gave us an opportunity to work on language arts skills. We wrote thank-you notes to people who contributed tabs, sent letters with newspaper articles about our project to friends, and mailed business letters to companies that bottled soft drinks. Students wrote about the project in their journals. Following each of our expeditions, I wrote a morning message describing the activity and including the names of the students who participated. The class then marked such features of my message as parts of speech, syllables, phrases, and clauses.

In addition to its connections to academic instruction, our project revealed many interesting feelings as well. If we don't reach our goal, are we good or bad? Should I ask my grouchy neighbor to save tabs? Feelings of competition arose when Jaime collected more tabs than anyone. All of us felt discouraged at times. But we discussed our feelings openly, and our class motto, "I Can Do Anything," helped ease the feelings of discouragement.

To keep spirits high, we set up a "goodie box" from which the top collector of the week could choose a prize. A parent gave us a Christmas tree made of 226 tabs. We took slides of our activities in anticipation of making a slide presentation when we reached our goal. We played host to visitors, ranging from the superintendent and the principal to three school board members and two reporters. Articles subsequently appeared in the *Phoenix Gazette* and the *Glendale Star*.

Our original goal was to see what a million looked like. However, as we were collecting the tabs, we found that some people didn't want to give them up. They were planning to donate to the Arizona Kidney Foundation the money they raised from recycling the tabs. We voted to do the same. Two speakers from the foundation came to our room with a slide presentation and information on dialysis.

Just before Christmas vacation, we received word that a local television station was interested in reporting about our project. The television crew came in January to shoot the story. After this publicity, we received tabs from organizations and individuals in such Arizona cities as Winslow and Peoria. On February 27 we received the final 230 pounds of tabs that put us over the top.

At our victory party, we ate cookies shaped like pull tabs, watched a slide presentation, and talked with visitors from the media. Students recorded their thoughts for a classroom book; later, for parents and pull-tab donors, we presented a program in the school library that featured the pile of one million tabs we had worked so hard to collect.

Update — *Ms. Walker concedes that only strongly motivated teachers should take on projects of the sort described in her article. She notes that "a friend tried our project but gave it up when she saw it was a lot of work. Also, she was married and had family obligations." Another Phoenix teacher sponsored a similar project but did not reach the goal of one million.*

Last year Ms. Walker's class of fourth-graders adopted a cheetah at the Phoenix Zoo. In order to do this, the children collected $430 in pennies. They also collected pledges for a 100-mile bike trip Ms. Walker took. "Our total," says Ms. Walker, "was $1,387, the most collected by any school for the Adopt-an-Animal Program for the zoo."

Editor's Note — *Ms. Walker's class sold the pull tabs they collected to a recycling firm, and the proceeds were given to the Arizona Kidney Foundation. State kidney foundations cannot accept pull tabs directly. Teachers should make sure of the market for collections of this kind before adopting a project.*

Fresh Curriculum and Teaching Strategies

A Team Approach to American Studies

by **Marion Bench** (November 1982)

What's twice as good as taking either American literature or American history? Walter Myers, a sophomore at Valhalla High School in El Cajon, California, thinks that the answer is enrolling in the team-taught, interdisciplinary American Studies program at his school. With a little money and a lot of energy, other high schools can find out whether or not he's right.

The seven-year-old American Studies program at Valhalla blends American history and literature and is taught by a team of six teachers, three of whom teach in the program full time. A group of teachers designed the program to emphasize the cross-disciplinary quality of the humanities.

The year-long program includes six units, each six weeks in duration: westward movement; power to the people; individuals in America; man and machine; war, peace, and protest; and American dream, thought, and value. There are three classes daily, each two hours long (divided into three 40-minute periods). Some 450 sophomores now take part in the program, which is conducted in a large pod of rooms that accommodates up to 200 students or can be broken down into smaller spaces.

The format of the classes varies from small seminars to large-group lectures; occasional films, guest speakers, and simulations augment these more traditional forms of instruction. The leader of the teaching team works out a weekly schedule, which might require students to attend, for example, a history lecture, a literature lecture, a film, and seminars.

Because four of the six team members are always teaching in the program at any given time, students have a measure of choice. Moreover, the combined skills and talents of six teachers insure that students will receive the best instruction that the school has to offer. For example, a teacher with a specialty in creative writing might teach the same seminar on poetry several

---

Marion Bench is the current team leader of the American Studies program at Valhalla High School, El Cajon, Calif.

times to different groups of students; another teacher with a strong background in drama might conduct the seminars on plays.

History and literature go well together. For example, in the unit on power to the people, students read writings of Benjamin Franklin, Patrick Henry, and Thomas Jefferson, along with short stories such as "The Ambitious Guest," by Nathaniel Hawthorne, and "The Lottery," by Shirley Jackson; plays such as *The Crucible*, by Arthur Miller; poems such as "The People Speak," by Carl Sandburg; and the novel *In Dubious Battle*, by John Steinbeck. During the unit on war, peace, and protest, students study the major U.S. wars as presented by a history textbook. At the same time, they read Ernest Hemingway's *Farewell to Arms* and Stephen Crane's *Red Badge of Courage*.

One of the benefits of an interdisciplinary course that is team taught is the creative thinking that emerges from group planning sessions. The "trials project" in the power to the people unit grew out of the suggestion of a teacher with a legal background that students could research and re-enact significant trials. The project requires students to conduct research, write reports, and perform the re-enactment. The re-enactment of the Chicago Eight trial was used as a segment on a local television news show.

Despite the happy marriage of the subject matters of history and literature and the enhanced creativity of six minds planning together, the program has not been entirely free of trouble. The psychological stress of having to reach a weekly consensus on how to approach each topic can be grueling, according to Marianne Johnson, who taught in the program for five years and served as team leader for two. Yet, by discussion and compromise, she points out, the team must find "a common thread that all the teachers will agree upon."

Dan Pumphrey, currently director of the Regional Occupation Program for the Grossmont (California) Union High School District, remembers that some teachers were not always compatible with others, that students were sometimes confused by the scheduling, and that students were occasionally reluctant to accept the responsibility that the program places on them. He also believes that provision must be made to allow teachers who are tired of the pace of team teaching to leave the program, at least for a time, and be replaced by fresh troops.

Pumphrey suggests the following eight guidelines for schools that wish to set up interdisciplinary programs similar to the American Studies program at Valhalla:

• Find out what is being done elsewhere. Pumphrey visited schools in Connecticut, Maryland, Pennsylvania, New York, New Jersey, and Vir-

117

ginia to watch small teaching teams at work. Usually these teams consisted of only two teachers; the six-person Valhalla team is recruited from the entire district.

- Find teachers who believe in the idea. Team teaching takes more time and energy than regular teaching. Thus teachers must be strongly committed to the value of the idea.

- Obtain administrative and faculty support. Because the course requires two hours daily, planning the master schedule requires the cooperation of the administration and other faculty members. The teaching team also must share the same free periods for planning.

- Develop themes for the units. The thematic approach helps to focus an interdisciplinary program.

- Develop curricula. During one summer, six teachers collaborated on a course outline, collected readings, devised independent activities, and coordinated related media. All of their work came together in a curriculum guide.

- Build or find flexible space. Flexible programs with variable formats and class sizes operate best in flexible space.

- Provide alternative approaches for those few students who are unable to handle the interdisciplinary approach. Some students, whose skills are below average or who are continually frustrated and confused, will need alternatives.

- Sell the program to the community. Involve parents directly in teaching, grading, or working with small groups. Parents also can be very effective guest lecturers.

In 1979, partly because of its interdisciplinary approach, Valhalla High School was selected as one of 15 schools in the U.S. to be affiliated with the National Humanities Faculty, which is subsidized by the National Endowment for the Humanities. David Haliburton of Stanford University, a National Humanities Faculty consultant, believes that the program at Valhalla offers "a good blend of variety (a wide range of teaching and learning modes), continuity (block sessions and interconnections between units), and organization (strong themes and appropriate pacing)." The faculty and students at Valhalla share his enthusiasm.

Update — *Ms. Bench writes that American Studies is alive and flourishing at Valhalla High School after 12 years. (It was seven years old when she wrote this article.) There have been minor changes. The program is now taught by five instead of six teachers, partly because of a modest decrease in the number of sophomores who take it.*

A more important change is the creation of a Living History Project, inaugurated by two librarians in 1982. In the project, each sophomore is matched with senior citizens. *The students interview persons who have lived through some important event or period: the Great Depression, the two World Wars, the age of rapid technological development, etc. This project has attracted national interest and results annually in newspaper and media attention.*

Not only is the program still supported with enthusiasm, Ms. Bench writes, but it continues to win awards. The Valhalla Library/Media Center was selected for a Golden Bell Award from the California School Boards Association, the first such award granted a high school library in the state. The library program undergirds the entire humanities cross-disciplinary program.

Starting the Day with a Good Book

by Lois Distad (February 1987)

A year ago last October, I stood at the window before the school day began, watching the children on the playground. One child huddled against a pole, her cold, bare hands tucked into the sleeves of her coat. Another slumped against the building wall — a punishment for having tripped a classmate.

As I watched these children, I wondered why we could not make better use of their time. Why not, for instance, spare them the exposure to the Wyoming winter and let them read instead? Why not open a reading lab every day before school? Outside, they belonged to the playground; inside, they would belong to me. I asked myself whether I could afford to give up my own preparation time to supervise such a program. But a better question was, Could I afford not to?

I began my planning for the lab in the fall of 1985. First, I spoke to the special education teacher, who agreed that the idea was a good one. We adapted a series of incentives that she had developed to maintain student interest. After 15 visits to the lab, students would receive a bookmark. Another 35 visits would earn them a button; 50 more visits would entitle them to a book; for readers still with the program after 100 days, a surprise party would be held. As they entered the lab each day, we decided to stamp the students' hands, so that they could show classmates and teachers that they had visited the lab. Stamping hands also would give teachers who supervised the lab a chance to greet students individually and pass on words of support.

Next, I set specific goals for the lab:

- to give all students, from kindergarten through grade 6, the opportunity to read independently every day;

Lois Distad is a reading specialist at Bar Nunn Elementary School in Casper, Wyo.

- to create a positive learning environment in which students could realize that reading is an enjoyable experience;
- to build cohesive relationships among students and teachers by sharing reading time every day; and
- to enhance students' self-esteem by encouraging their participation and showing approval of their reading activities.

Finally, to create some structure, I created a set of rules for the lab:

1. For 20 minutes before the morning bell, students and staff would be welcome to bring books or magazines to read in the lab (held in our school library). A variety of literature also would be available.
2. Participants could sit anywhere, although intermediate students would be encouraged to sit on one side of the room and primary students on the other. (Young children frequently read aloud, and this can disturb older, silent readers.)
3. No visiting would be permitted. (Children who could not control themselves would be asked to leave and be encouraged to return the next day.)
4. To prevent them from wandering in the halls, students would be allowed to enter the building through one outside door only.
5. Participants would be required to remain in the lab until the first bell.

Armed with a copy of *Becoming a Nation of Readers*, I called a staff meeting to see whether my colleagues would be willing to help with the lab. I planned to remind them that the Commission on Reading of the National Academy of Education had stated that "the amount of independent, silent reading children do in school is significantly related to gains in reading achievement" and that "the amount of reading students do out of school is consistently related to gains in achievement." The commission also recommended that "two hours a week of independent reading should be expected by the time children are in third or fourth grade. To do this, children need ready access to books and guidance in choosing appropriate and interesting books."

I was prepared to argue that, if we encourage children to read for fun every day while they are at school, they might more often choose books over television at home. I planned to remind the other teachers that we frequently encourage parents to read to and in front of their children, but we don't spend much time ourselves modeling reading in our classrooms. The 20 minutes before school each morning would give us a perfect opportunity to do so.

I never had to use my arguments. Thirteen teachers and two aides (out of 18 regular staff members) immediately volunteered their time.

We opened the doors of the reading lab in November 1985. On the first day, we drew 150 students. Since that first week, 230 students out of our total enrollment of 272 have visited the morning lab. The 15 staff members have constructed a weekly schedule, so two or three adults can be found reading in the lab each morning.

Now in its second year, the Bar Nunn Elementary School reading lab runs smoothly. Organizers have found it to be a simple way to turn "extra" minutes into a reading partnership that illustrates how seriously the school regards its commitment to promote students' academic and emotional growth.

Update — *Ms. Distad writes that the reading lab described in this article, now in its third year, is a solid, successful program appreciated by students, parents, administrators, and teachers.*

Only two changes have occurred. First, student incentives now vary from year to year to maintain interest. However, every year a student can earn at least three books in addition to bookmarks, pencils, book plates, a surprise party, and other rewards. Second, the lab has evolved into a reading/writing lab. Each morning two tables are equipped with lined paper, pencils, and pictures that encourage students to write. In the 1987-88 school year Bar Nunn Elementary was awarded a $10,000 "Super Schools" grant to improve student writing skills. Says Ms. Distad, "Because every child in every classroom writes every day, their competence and enthusiasm are now happily visible in the lab as well."

Fifty to 150 students visit the lab daily. Almost 90% of the students in the school attend at least once. More than 50% attend at least 15 times. And some students attend 170 of the required 177 school days. Each year, student attendance has increased.

Ms. Distad received approximately 100 requests for more information about the Bar Nunn reading program after the Kappan *article appeared. She has helped secondary teachers to adapt the program to the needs of junior high and high school students.*

Westward Movement in American History Is Re-created in 'Boomsville' in Bellport

by Laile E. Fairbairn, David Tiffany, and Joseph Intonato (March 1983)

For the past 12 years, four fifth-grade classes at the Hampton Avenue Intermediate School in Bellport, New York, have spent a year in an imaginary town called Boomsville. Over the course of the year, the students build the town, buy and sell land, and set up their own monetary system. They research and establish their own businesses and industries and develop and market their own products. They also buy and sell bonds, money-market certificates, and precious metals; invest in stocks; and trade in commodities.

The Hampton Avenue Intermediate School houses all the fourth- and fifth-graders in the South Country School District, a racially mixed district some 60 miles east of New York City on Long Island. The Boomsville project has been run by a team of four teachers. Full-scale planning sessions were held each day during the first year, but these have since given way to detailed planning for entire units, with only a brief team meeting held each morning. In addition, before the start of each day's classwork, a short "town meeting" is held to inform the students of the upcoming activities. The teachers encourage the elected town officials to run these meetings.

Each area of the fifth-grade curriculum is integrated into the program, whose unifying theme is the westward movement in U.S. history. Through the detailed re-creation of a small town, students learn the workings of a market economy; they learn to make decisions about buying and selling; even science projects can be incorporated into the Boomsville experience. The children also write, edit, and print their own newspaper.

Each fall the project begins with each child building a model of a covered wagon in which he or she will transport a family to Boomsville. Dur-

At the time this article was written, Laile E. Fairbairn was principal of the Hampton Avenue Intermediate School in Bellport, N.Y. She currently is director of instruction in the South Country Central School District, East Patchogue, N.Y. David Tiffany and Joseph Intonato are fifth-grade teachers in the Hampton Avenue Intermediate School and originators of the Boomsville project.

ing this period the children are busy saving "smurgwoskers" — play money that they can earn by good academic performance, good behavior, or helping with classroom chores.

The wagon train leaves for Boomsville in early November. Each student is the skipper of his or her own prairie schooner, and the wagon train winds across the playground and comes to rest in a circle round a campfire, where the children enjoy "buffalo" stew and roasted potatoes. This feast is followed by games and square dancing; afterward the "Boomers" return to their classroom, which has officially become Boomsville, their new home.

Each of the 250 ceiling tiles of the classroom represents a parcel of land in Boomsville. All the new Boomers take part in a lottery, at which time the parcels are distributed, one to a customer. The undistributed property is reserved for later sale. The children have one month to construct a house on their property or risk losing the land. An election is held, and the Boomers select their town officials, including the town leader, the Boommeister.

The town itself consists of a Main Street, surrounded by large cardboard buildings constructed from boxes obtained from the school cafeteria over a number of years. These buildings are large enough for students to walk into, and they include a post office, a bank, an assay office, a real estate office, an insurance office, a saloon, a patent office, and a general store. Students visit Main Street on designated days to conduct their business. For example, test papers and student folders can be turned in at the assay office in exchange for smurgwoskers, which students can then use to purchase unsold ceiling lots. Postal workers distribute the corrected assignments.

Students are encouraged to create products from the scrap materials that are sold throughout the town. They also can obtain patents to protect their rights to their products. When enough products have become available, the Marketplace is born. On Marketplace Day, students congregate in the center of town to sell their products for smurgwoskers.

Meanwhile, Uptown Boomsville (the ceiling) continues to develop; and before long all the available land has been sold. The eastern part of Uptown represents the East Coast of the U.S., and some of this land is reserved for business property. The center of the ceiling represents the Midwest and is mainly reserved for farming. The western part of Uptown represents the dry plains of the West, where a student must hold three adjoining parcels of land in order to establish a ranch. The value of the land in the West is lower than in other regions, because the area lacks adequate rainfall.

But the value of that western land might increase greatly if some unsuspected mineral resources should be discovered there. Before any of the land is distributed, the teachers have hidden just such "discoveries," scattered at random on a master chart before the children arrive for the fall semester. On Discovery Days, the children learn whether the land they have purchased contains deposits of gold, silver, iron ore, copper, oil, or other valuable minerals. The discovery of mineral wealth increases the value of the land and entitles the owner to a cash bonus as well.

During the course of the year, houses, barns, fences, and windmills are purchased and suspended from the parcels of land on the ceiling. The ceiling becomes a colorful addition to the classroom, as oil derricks, open-pit mines, forests, mountains, airports, and bridges are added. Farmers purchase seed, fertilizer, and livestock to increase the value of their land. The children also are encouraged to purchase insurance against disasters; a certain number of fires, floods, tornadoes, and so forth are sure to befall some property owners in Boomsville during the year.

In the spring, the town changes from an agricultural to an industrial society. Students select businesses, research their choices, and build model buildings to hang from selected business property on the ceiling. Each successful business is entitled to become a part of the Boomsville Stock Market.

When the Stock Market opens, two phases of Boomsville — the Marketplace and Main Street — end. The buildings are taken down, and the stock exchange and the commodity market go into operation. Children also are urged to invest their savings in municipal bonds and money-market certificates.

Springtime brings re-enactments of famous events in American history. These re-enactments take place on the playground and have included such events as the Gold Rush, the construction of the transcontinental railroad, and the building of the Erie Canal.

At the end of the school year, each student tallies up his or her assets for the year. The students discover that, just as in real life, some have become wealthy and others have gone broke. The student who has amassed the most money is named "Boomer of the Year." On the final report card, each student is given a grade for participation in "Boomsville."

The Boomsville project has grown and prospered from year to year — under the leadership of three different principals with three different leadership styles. It has meant some extra work for teachers — giving up a lunch period occasionally to supervise construction, videotaping a play, or hosting a Boomsville open house on parents' night. But the extra efforts have been worthwhile, for they have helped bring to life a page of American history.

Update — *The Boomsville project is still alive and well in the Hampton Avenue School, writes Ms. Fairbairn. However, since the fifth-grade social studies curriculum is no longer based strictly on history, Mr. Intonato has modified the project. Instead of the class moving westward during the course of the year, they live on a tropical island.*

American Studies at Central High

by Jane Ingram, Kenneth T. Henson, and Adolph B. Crew (December 1984)

What can a school do to generate enthusiasm among students in nonbasic courses? In the American Studies Program at Central High School in Tuscaloosa, Alabama, students look forward to going to jail.

The American Studies Program was conceived in response to a 1979 federal court ruling that achieved racial desegregation by pairing two recently built segregated high schools. While this measure successfully eliminated the segregated schools, many people felt that it did so at the expense of the students' community identity. And many students did indeed respond to the ruling with apathy. The level of participation in school activities decreased, while absenteeism soared.

A committee of teachers, administrators, and faculty members from the University of Alabama concluded that participation in community life would diminish feelings of alienation among the students. The American Studies Program they designed is housed in the Old Jail, which is located in Tuscaloosa's historical district. The program provides students with a sense of community, gives them reason to explore their *uncommon* heritage, involves them in preservation of the area's history, and requires them to participate in the political life of the city.

The program began in 1980 with 145 juniors and seniors and has continued to grow. The staff includes a director and three teachers who team-teach in a four-hour block each morning. The students return to the main campus for classes each afternoon.

Flexible scheduling allows students to attend town meetings, seminars, and labs and to participate in extended field trips. The films, lectures, and

Jane Ingram is a teacher in the American Studies Program at Central High School, Tuscaloosa, Ala. When this article was written in 1984, Kenneth T. Henson was professor and head of the Department of Curriculum and Instruction at the University of Alabama, Tuscaloosa. He now is dean of the College of Education at Eastern Kentucky University. Adolph B. Crew is professor and head of the Social Science Program, College of Education, University of Alabama, Tuscaloosa.

performances that students attend in the program are followed by seminars attended by 25 to 30 students. The labs are designed to focus on the skills in reading, writing, speaking, and problem solving that are required for specific tasks.

The courses for the juniors — American history, American literature, writing, and environmental science — emphasize historical preservation. The students are encouraged to familiarize themselves with the many resources available through the University of Alabama and the local junior college and from the citizens of Tuscaloosa. Some students research local history, using genealogies, oral histories, and data from their own architectural survey. Another group forms the staff of *Timepiece*, a student publication that features project-related articles, interviews, family stories, and local tall tales.

Students also visit Tanglewood, a 480-acre plantation donated to the university in 1949. The mansion, built in 1858, contains documents dating back as far as 1819 that provide fascinating insights into the history of a Southern family. The original land grant, signed by President Martin Van Buren, hangs on one wall beside two original bills of sale for slaves. Students camp out on the grounds of the estate, using only equipment that would have been available in the mid-19th century. Such activities encourage cooperation and a sense of community among the students.

The seniors' course of study is broader. It revolves around participation in the national political process. Students form their own government and explore such themes as the struggle to survive (frontier and wilderness), the struggle to cooperate (the formation of government, with emphasis on the executive branch), the struggle to create (the legislative branch), and the struggle to justify (the judicial branch).

Significant contemporary events are used as peak experiences in the curriculum. Local, state, and national elections provide students with a variety of opportunities through which they can investigate the American political process. Some students volunteer to work in the campaign headquarters of the party or candidate of their choice. Candidates and their campaign organizers visit the classroom and describe the electoral process to the seniors. Appropriate literature, such as Robert Penn Warren's *All the King's Men*, helps to relate classroom work to field study.

The seniors also study and employ propaganda techniques in a mock debate and election. They learn to analyze the arguments offered on opposing sides of controversial issues and to write position papers on the issues. As a community service, on the day after an election, students collect every visible campaign poster within the city limits. The culminating experience of the senior semester is an extended field trip to Washington, D.C.

There are many important advantages to the American Studies Program. Perhaps the most important is that it provides an opportunity for personal growth. Students learn to look at experience as multifaceted, to make judgments from a broader base, and to bring their own heritage into clearer focus. For many, this method of perceiving experience and making judgments will become a habit. The experiential nature of the program necessitates firsthand learning by the students. Because they are given tasks that require cooperation, they have developed a sense of community by the end of the semester. At the same time, their personal investment in these tasks motivates students to improve their basic skills in reading, writing, speaking, and problem solving.

Thanks to its popularity and record of success, the American Studies Program has become a permanent part of the Tuscaloosa curriculum. An officer of the Southeastern American Studies Association described Tuscaloosa's program as "the most extensive and challenging application of American Studies in the high school that has ever been attempted anywhere in the country." The team of American Studies teachers at Central High School has found the experience both time- and energy-consuming but professionally fulfilling. The students, too, have found that the program requires extra time and effort. But there is general agreement among all the participants that the quality of the experience makes it worthwhile.

Update — Mr. Henson writes that, after seven years, the American Studies Program at Central High is as vigorous as ever. There has been little turnover in its teachers, and it remains a volunteer program that students choose over the traditional social studies program.

There has been one change in operational procedure. Initially, the teachers returned in the afternoons to Central High to teach. They no longer do so. The program has been expanded to include elementary children, who come to the jail in the afternoons for instruction by the same teachers who teach high school students in the morning.

Mr. Henson observes that the Central High American Studies Program could be successfully transplanted to almost any school. The only essential ingredient is a few people who are interested in the heritage of their community or region. Politicians can be very supportive. Historical societies can contribute. University or college faculty in science, social studies, and English can become involved. Mr. Henson notes that the Central High program has been described at conventions of both the National Council of Teachers of English and the National Council for the Social Studies.

Two-Way Instructional Television

by William B. Kested (December 1985)

Can a small rural school district offer courses in advanced mathematics, foreign languages, and shorthand if the enrollment in each course is only three to five students? Normally, the answer would be no. But four school districts in Carroll County, Illinois, have developed a system of cooperative teaching by means of two-way instructional television that enables them to offer courses in advanced mathematics, shorthand, and Spanish I, II, and III.

In 1982 the Shannon, Lanark, Milledgeville, and Chadwick school districts began a dialogue on ways to combat declining enrollments and dwindling state and federal funds without giving up advanced courses for highly motivated students. The administrators and school board members from each district traveled to Trempealleau County, Wisconsin, to observe an existing instructional television system.

This visit sparked discussion of an area instructional television system among administrators, boards of education, and the Illinois State Board of Education. When the state board agreed to sanction a five-year experimental system, the four high schools formed the Carroll Instructional Television Consortium.

Each school designated one classroom as a television studio. Each district purchased color cameras, microphones, a video recorder, a special effects generator/switcher, and color monitors. This one-time purchase of equipment cost each district between $10,000 and $18,000. (The variance in cost was due to differences in equipment and in the cost of remodeling the rooms.) A lease agreement with the area cable television company was made, in which the cable company agreed to provide eight channels for five years at an annual cost of $1,645 per district.

When this article was written in 1985, William B. Kested was assistant principal of Shannon (Ill.) High School. He now is principal of the Orangeville, Ill., Junior-Senior High School.

130

In order to enroll in a television class, a student and his or her parents must sign a contract in which the student and the parents agree that, if the student disrupts the television class for any reason, he or she may be dropped from the class and barred from re-entry. In most of the consortium schools, no teacher or aide is present when the school receives a transmission of a class from another school. If a disruption does occur, the teacher in the sending school telephones the receiving school and reports the incident; the local administrator then takes appropriate disciplinary action.

Teachers are selected for television teaching according to a number of criteria, including collegiate training in the subject area, years of teaching experience, past evaluations, and desire to teach via the television system. Once the teachers are selected, they participate in an inservice training program that teaches them how to operate the equipment.

Unlike many educational television projects, the Carroll Consortium is a two-way system. Up to 16 classes per school can be accommodated on the system, and two separate classes can be taught simultaneously. While a teacher in one school teaches a class in the usual fashion, students in as many as three other schools may also take the class. The cameras and microphones in the sending school allow students in the receiving schools to watch and listen to the class. Cameras and microphones in the receiving schools allow students there to be seen and heard by the teacher and by all the other students (in whatever school they may be). A question asked by a student in a remote site can be heard and answered as if the student and the teacher were in the same room.

Each school's studio classroom is arranged in essentially the same manner. One camera, placed behind the teacher, is aimed at the students; a second camera, placed behind the students, is aimed at the teacher; a third camera is mounted on a pole attached to the teacher's desk. This desk-mounted camera records such close-up operations as the solving of math problems on paper or the proper formation of a shorthand symbol.

The special effects generator/switcher allows the teacher to use a split-screen and other combinations of images. For example, the advanced math teacher can put an image of himself in the upper left-hand corner of the television screen, so that the students at the remote sites can see him, while the remainder of the screen is filled by the paper on which he is demonstrating the solution to a math problem.

Other benefits of the system include the fact that all lessons can be videotaped, so that students who have been absent can view any lessons they missed. Lessons also can be taped in advance, if an instructor will be unable to be present in the classroom. Videotapes also can be used by teachers for self-criticism or peer review of their performance.

Tests and other papers are easily exchanged between and among the schools, since most of the schools have at least one teacher who lives in another of the school districts in the consortium. Occasionally, some papers must be transported first to one school and then sent from there to their final destination.

With the possible expansion of the system into adult education, general community service, and inservice training for teachers, the Carroll Instructional Television Consortium offers additional opportunities for cooperation among the four communities. In the spring of 1985, for example, Highland Community College, in Freeport, Illinois, offered a course in computer theory over the system. The possibilities for further expansion of the system to include other schools and communities outside the consortium are boundless.

Update — *Mr. Kested reports that the consortium he described is alive and well. The sole focus now is foreign language. Currently, two years of French and four of Spanish are taught with the two-way instructional television system. Mr. Kested notes that other districts have shown interest in developing similar systems. Generally, these districts have several high schools and are concerned with providing instruction in highly theoretical courses such as advanced physics and low-enrollment classes such as second-year calculus. Inquiries about the system should now be addressed to Joel McFadden, Superintendent, Eastland CUSD #308, Lanark, IL 61046.*

The Open-Lab Period: A Schedule That Promotes Individualized Instruction

by Judson A. Morhart (May 1982)

Many teachers are frustrated by the obstacles that rigid class schedules place in the way of small-group or individualized instruction. Students in need of extra help or those who wish to pursue special interests are unlikely to be free at the same times. Nor are their teachers apt to have conveniently scheduled free periods. Moreover, many students have after-school responsibilities — extracurricular activities, part-time jobs, or bus departure schedules to meet.

At Pueblo Junior High School in Los Alamos, New Mexico, we have developed the open-lab period to reduce these frustrations. The open lab affords teachers the opportunity to adjust their instruction to the needs of small groups of students. It also gives students the chance to pursue special interests.

The open-lab period grew out of a modular schedule that was scrapped by Pueblo Junior High School in the early Seventies. The open lab offers a measure of control that was missing in the modular system and at the same time frees students and teachers from an inflexible schedule. Twice each week, on Tuesdays and Thursdays, rearrangement of the regular schedule creates a free period. But two controlling mechanisms prevent the system from degenerating into anarchy.

The first controlling mechanism is the open-lab pass. These passes are simply theater tickets, purchased in bulk and stamped with the name of a teacher.

Teachers may give students passes for the open-lab period for a variety of reasons. For example, an English teacher might give passes to three second-period students, one fourth-period student, and two seventh-period students, all of whom are having difficulty with transitive verbs. A science

---

When this article was written in 1982, Judson A. Morhart was principal of Pueblo Junior High School in Los Alamos, N.M. He is now coordinator of instruction for the Los Alamos schools.

teacher might give students passes so that they can make up lab experiments under close supervision. A social studies teacher might allow students to make up a missed test during the lab period. Each teacher keeps a list of the students to whom he or she has issued passes. Students may also request passes to work on subjects in which they need special help or to pursue special interests.

Only one pass may be used during an open-lab period, however. And a teacher's demand pass takes precedence over a student's request pass. If two teachers issue passes to the same student for the same period, the teachers must work out the problem between themselves.

The second mechanism of control is the house group — an organization somewhat like a homeroom but with no connection to the first-period class. Students in each grade are assigned randomly to house advisors. All full-time teachers are advisors, so the ratio of students to advisors is about 22 to 1. At the beginning of each open-lab period, all students report to their house advisors, who check students' passes and release them to the teachers or activities that they have scheduled.

Arranging the free time for the open-lab period is not difficult. On the first day scheduled for an open-lab period, the eighth-period class is simply dropped from the schedule and replaced by the open lab. On the second day, the seventh-period class is dropped, and the eighth-period class moves to the seventh period — thus freeing the last period of the day for the open lab. A special schedule accommodates class periods that alternate with lunch periods. When each of the afternoon classes has been dropped once, we begin dropping morning classes, each in its turn, and schedule the open lab for the last period before lunch. When the cycle is completed, we start over again.

Flexibility is the hallmark of the open-lab plan. It can begin at any time during the school year. However, our experience suggests that it is wise to wait until the regular schedule of classes is running smoothly before instituting the open-lab period. Scheduling of the open-lab period can be changed to accommodate holidays, school assemblies, or special performances. Moreover, if needs change, the open-lab period is easily discontinued without disrupting anyone's schedule.

The open-lab period allows structured regrouping of students and teachers for individualized and small-group instruction. It provides closer teacher/student contact for remedial work, special projects, make-up assignments and tests, and accelerated study programs. And it does all of these things at minimal cost. Fifty dollars will cover the cost of blank theater tickets; the rest of the program requires only skillful organization.

Update — *Mr. Morhart writes that the open-lab concept of individualizing instruction is still functioning in his district. Although Pueblo Junior High has been closed, its student body, many of its faculty, and the structure of the open lab were transferred to the new Los Alamos Middle School. The open lab program's name has been changed to STRETCH, an acronym for Student Teacher Review Enrichment Test Club and Help Session, and the program is scheduled weekly instead of bi-weekly.*

The program continues to provide greater flexibility to the normal school day and closer student/teacher contact. It provides time during the school day for students to 1) make up tests and science labs, 2) get individual help from a teacher during the day on a difficult topic, 3) pursue special interests such as student government or pep club, and 4) go to the library to conduct research for term papers or special projects. Teachers use the STRETCH period to regroup students for remedial work and to structure small-group sessions for students in need of acceleration. The controlling mechanisms — tickets to schedule students into the STRETCH period and the teacher advisor program to control the location of students during the period — are key elements of continued success.

STRETCH was recently chosen as the first-place winner in the division for school districts with 3,000 to 5,000 students in the Quality Education Award Program of the New Mexico Research and Study Council. More than 150 New Mexico schools competed for the awards, which have cash as well as prestige value.

A Reading Program
That Works as a Community Effort

by Mary R. McGrath (February 1987)

When Samuel Bowles School in Springfield, Massachusetts, began its Reading Incentive Program in 1983, the primary goal was to encourage students to read. Incentives lured students to the library, where volunteer listeners not only kept tabs on them but also worked to promote intelligent conversation about books in an informal atmosphere.

The incentives were simple. Each student who read and reported on a book received a certificate redeemable at a local ice cream store. When a student completed 12 books, a new book was placed in the school library with a bookplate announcing it as the gift of that reader.

Arranging for listeners was a bit more complicated. But over the years, volunteers had helped the school in various ways, so we had a foundation on which to build. Letters to parents describing the program yielded several recruits. We also contacted retired teachers, librarians, church groups, and friends and neighbors of Bowles School. We eventually recruited about 40 listeners, who later attended a workshop acquainting them with the program.

We asked each volunteer to spend at least one hour each week conversing with a student. The day and time were arranged with the child's teacher. To keep disruption to a minimum, the regularly scheduled library period was often used for conversations. To get around children's negative feelings about book reports, we made the reports oral and informal. It soon became common to see an adult and a child in a corner of the library or in a corridor animatedly discussing a book. Each time a child reported on a book, the volunteer recorded relevant data.

Although we used extrinsic rewards to attract children to the library, we hoped that they would gradually develop an interest in reading and become self-motivated. This hope has been realized. Though incentives are used

---

Mary R. McGrath is principal of Samuel Bowles School, Springfield, Mass.

only during the first semester of each school year, the children continue — and even increase — their reading during the second semester. Participation in the program has grown from 320 youngsters in 1983 to 400 youngsters today. The participants range in age from kindergartners (who are not yet able to read independently) to fourth-graders. Some are bilingual; some have special learning needs.

We attribute the success of the Reading Incentive Program to several factors. The friendly, nonthreatening setting promotes open and eager discussions of books. The adult listeners, though usually lacking formal training for this task, intuitively ask questions that stimulate such skills as drawing conclusions, detecting absurdities, and making inferences. The individual attention ensures that students are developing appropriate study skills and thought processes.

For a child whose native tongue is English, this is a golden opportunity to talk and be listened to. For a child who speaks English as a second language, it is an opportunity to practice new language skills in a pressure-free environment. For a child who lacks attention at home, it is a rare opportunity to converse with a friendly adult. There is nothing contrived about these conversations. They unfold quite naturally, and that is the program's strength.

The investment of time and effort has paid excellent dividends. The Reading Incentive Program has proved to be simple and workable. It has received excellent support from both staff and parents, and volunteers continue to gain satisfaction from their efforts. Both the local and the school libraries have noted increased circulation since the program's founding. Most important, however, is the marked improvement in reading skills, particularly among reluctant readers. Because of the Reading Incentive Program, Bowles students will leave elementary school with stronger reading skills, greater self-esteem, and the knowledge that reading is enjoyable.

Update — *Ms. McGrath writes that the reading program described in this article has been adopted in the past year by more than 20 Springfield schools and has been copied by schools elsewhere in Massachusetts as well as in Connecticut, Virginia, and Florida. She adds, "To teach children how to read is a noble calling, but to communicate to children the idea that reading is fun is to offer a lovely and long-lasting gift."*

Creative Writing and Storytelling: A Bridge from High School to Preschool

by Joseph Sanacore (March 1983)

Although writing stories and telling them are distinct processes, they are clearly complementary. In the Hauppauge (New York) School District, we have blended the two into one unit of an elective course in creative writing, in which high school seniors write and illustrate stories and tell them to preschool children.

The writing that the seniors undertake in this course runs the gamut of short stories, poems, and plays. Some students even complete novellas. The seniors also prepare manuscripts for publication and select and develop markets for their work. Thus most of the content is just what one would expect in any creative writing course. The unit on composing and telling children's stories is different, however.

Before the students begin writing stories for children, they immerse themselves in published works of children's literature. This exposure helps them to identify and appreciate the story devices that professional writers use. Some of these devices also are transferable to the telling of stories. For example, much of the alliteration in Rudyard Kipling's *Just So Stories* is designed to involve listeners. By the same token, the repeated refrains in Esphyr Slobodkina's *Caps for Sale* and the incremental refrains in Ellen Raskin's *Ghost in a Four-Room Apartment* entice children to participate in the storytelling.

When the seniors begin writing their own stories, the teacher offers praise, provides suggestions for improvement, and encourages students to share ideas among themselves. Throughout, the emphasis is on improving the writing process rather than on correcting the written product. The prospect of a

Joseph Sanacore is English/reading coordinator (K-12) for the Hauppauge (New York) School District on Long Island. He acknowledges the support of creative writing teachers Teresa Nicodemi and Edward Wolfsohn, library/media center coordinator Caren Donnelly, and home economics/business education chairperson George Murphy.

real audience, eager to hear the stories, is both a valuable motivation for the seniors and a useful simulation of the working conditions of professional writers.

When the stories have been completed, students may volunteer to learn the techniques of storytelling and to tell their stories to preschoolers. Participation in this part of the creative writing course is optional. According to Kathryn Farnsworth, liking the story one plans to tell is a prerequisite to effective storytelling. Farnsworth writes: "Any misgivings or reservations you have about the story will be communicated to your listeners. So feeling that it is 'your' story comes first."[1] This advice fits well in the context of a creative writing course, since the stories that students volunteer to tell are truly their own.

Those students who do choose to be storytellers practice a variety of techniques. John Stewig offers excellent storytelling suggestions for teachers;[2] and in the Hauppauge creative writing program, we have adapted some of his suggestions for use with students:

• Students divide their plots into separate units of action and practice them in sequence. This does *not* mean that they memorize entire stories verbatim; rather, they learn the sequence of events.

• Students identify sections of their stories that *should* be memorized. For example, a repeated refrain that contributes significantly to the mood of the story should be committed to memory and incorporated word-for-word into the telling.

• Students develop fluency by practicing their deliveries about twice daily for at least a week prior to their performances. During these practice sessions, storytellers blend the memorized sections with the sequential units of action. Moreover, students must become accustomed to the sounds of their own voices. Thus they should rehearse in a comfortable environment — with friends or parents or alone in front of a mirror.

• Students monitor their progress by tape-recording the delivery of their stories. To gain some distance from their efforts, they wait several days before they listen to the tapes. Then they revise to achieve greater fluency, to sharpen certain parts of the stories, to clarify the mood, and to adjust such paralinguistic elements as tempo, pause, pitch, and so on.

The 3- and 4-year-olds to whom the high school storytellers tell their tales all are enrolled in the Child and Family Program of the Hauppauge School District. This program, sponsored by the Home Economics Department at Hauppauge High School, provides an opportunity for home economics students to learn about the physical, emotional, social, and intellectual development of young children. At the same time, the preschoolers derive benefits from a variety of activities, including listening to and participating in the storytelling.

As the seniors from the creative writing course tell their stories, the home economics students observe the children's behavior. Some of these activities are videotaped, so that the senior storytellers can evaluate their strengths and weaknesses. In addition, future students of creative writing can learn from videotapes of storytellers who have gone before. Some videotapes have been broadcast on local cable television channels, enabling members of the Hauppauge community to observe the creative interaction of the high school students and the preschoolers.

There are many benefits to this blend of creative writing and storytelling, both for the high school writers and for their preschool audience. The high school seniors enjoy writing and telling stories, and they also gain useful insights into related careers, such as public librarian, school library/media specialist, and writer/illustrator of children's books. The preschoolers become excited about the language and the plots of the stories. These experiences help to create in them the desire to read. Creative storytelling also provides opportunities for the children to become active participants in telling the stories and in acting out parts of them as they are being told. Such active participation is a satisfying experience for young children; it can also serve as an introduction to creative dramatics.

The relationship between the seniors and the preschoolers is genuinely warm and loving. This relationship provides the children with a positive introduction to school, and it gives the seniors a realistic perspective on the capacity of young children to use and appreciate language.

Copies of the stories are placed in the library/media center, where they are available for parents to use at home, for children to use independently, and for seniors in subsequent creative writing classes to refer to as models. The videotapes of storytelling also are available for parents' and students' use.

The creative writing and telling of children's stories have so far proved to be valuable links between the high school and the preschool. In the future, we plan to extend the storytelling to the elementary schools of the Hauppauge School District and to the pediatrics wards of local hospitals.

---

1. Kathryn Farnsworth, "Storytelling in the Classroom — Not an Impossible Dream," *Language Arts* (February 1981): 164.
2. John Warren Stewig, "Storyteller: Endangered Species?" *Language Arts* (March 1978): 339-45.

Update — *Mr. Sanacore writes:*

Since 1983 the Creative Writing and Child and Family Program described here has been regularly evaluated by a team of educators, who interview the preschoolers enrolled and survey their parents, as well as the seniors and teachers who participate. The evaluations support continuing the program. Among the findings:

- *Most of the preschool children read more books, self-select a wide variety of materials, maintain a desire to read, and tell their own stories.*
- *The vast majority of seniors increase their ability to communicate with a unique audience, the preschoolers. They also report improved awareness of children's ability to use and appreciate language.*

Educators who contemplate similar projects will find these sources valuable: Betty Coody, Using Literature with Young Children *(Wm. C. Brown); Bernice Culinan,* Children's Literature in the Reading Program *(International Reading Association); Edna Johnson et al.,* Anthology of Children's Literature *(Houghton Mifflin); John Warren Stewig,* Read to Write *(Holt, Rinehart, and Winston); Zena Sutherland,* The Arbuthnot Anthology of Children's Literature *(Scott, Foresman); and Sylvia Ziskind,* Telling Stories to Children *(H.W. Wilson).*

For Middle-Graders in East Elmhurst, 'Museum' Means School Learning Center

by Sidney Trubowitz and Clarence Bunch (February 1983)

To update this article, Mr. Trubowitz chose to make minor changes in the text.

The room is lit only by soft blue and red lights. Out of the darkness, suspended by strings from the ceiling, appears a giant, dark gray, blue-finned, papier-maché whale. Farther on there is a metal sculpture of a fish; and numerous straggly, multicolored, paper-and-ribbon mobiles dangle amid the sand and shells edging the walls. Posted all around are children's poems about the ocean and the life it holds. And through it all you hear the recorded sounds of waves breaking, of whales cooing, of water lapping the shore, and of music composed by children. You have entered a world of cool darkness, a world shaped by the imagination of children. You have entered "The Realms of the Sea," the latest exhibit of the Louis Armstrong School and Community Arts Museum.

For most schoolchildren a trip to the museum means a long bus ride, a race past exhibits (under the direction of a teacher urging silence), a museum guide attempting to do justice to the works of masters in mere seconds, and a gobbled lunch in a noisy, crowded cafeteria. Pupils at the Louis Armstrong Middle School in East Elmhurst, New York, have a different view of a museum, for they have one in their own school. The Louis Armstrong School and Community Arts Museum, an integral part of the school curriculum, is the result of a collaboration between the New York City Board of Education and Queens College. Learning at Louis Armstrong is not restricted to information gleaned from textbooks, nor need it take place only in a classroom.

Sidney Trubowitz is director of the Queens College Center for the Improvement of Education in the Middle Grades at Queens College, Flushing, N.Y., where Clarence Bunch is chairman of the Department of Secondary Education and Youth Services.

The museum has become a center for many kinds of learning. The inaugural exhibit, comprising etchings, cellotypes, and haiku poetry by children from Japan, led pupils to write their own haiku poems and to experiment with printmaking techniques taught to them in workshops conducted in the museum. In addition, one of the music teachers taught Japanese songs; and a home economics class prepared Japanese food. A future exhibit — paintings and drawings by middle-schoolers from the Soviet Union — will give students at Louis Armstrong an opportunity to learn about still another culture.

The museum has provided an opportunity to integrate subject matter from more than one discipline. For example, social studies teachers worked with students, student teachers, and an art education intern to convert the museum into the interior of an Egyptian tomb. The show, titled "You Can't Take It with You," joined the disciplines of art and social studies to describe life in ancient Egypt.

Children also visited the museum to view an exhibit on making a book and to learn the process of creating a book from Miriam Cohen, author of many children's books. She took them from the moment an idea found its way into her notebook to the time the finished book appeared in bookstores and was reviewed in magazines and newspapers. The children were intrigued by the prospect of meeting a "real" writer. Cohen (in her role as guest curator for the exhibit) and an art education intern trained a group of boys to serve as museum guides. These boys helped plan and install the exhibit. They also wrote and designed an attractive, informative catalogue.

The exhibit on making a book has begun to influence other schools. It has been shown at an elementary school in Queens and at a junior high school on Long Island and will soon travel to a middle school in California. It also has been displayed in two public libraries. From now on, at least one exhibit each year will become a public service loan exhibit. The college, too, has been affected, with students developing master's theses on the theme of a museum in the school and its impact on curriculum. Students also have found job opportunities as education directors in various museums.

Converting a public school classroom into a museum presents its own brand of problems. For example, we had to keep in mind the regulations of the New York City Board of Education. Physical fixtures of the museum were planned so that nothing was attached to a wall, and the room was not changed or defaced in any manner. To accomplish this we built a series of plywood display cases, four feet wide, eight feet tall, and 18 inches deep. One side of these cases is flat, designed to display drawings and paintings; the other side includes a 30-inch open case for displaying three-dimensional artworks. Above and below these three-dimensional display cases, the surface is flat, so that paintings and drawings may be displayed together with sculptures. When these units are placed side by side, they completely hide blackboards, lockers, and other classroom fixtures and create a room-within-a-room.

Using such units, simply and inexpensively made of pre-cut, standard-sized building materials, any school can easily create a museum in an empty classroom or in some other suitable space. It will be easily accessible to students, staff, and visitors; and the space can be arranged in many configurations.

The costs in terms of teacher time are also minimal. Each year an art education intern takes on the role of museum coordinator and is assisted by student teachers. An art teacher uses one of her class sessions to train students to be docents. Thus no extra expenses are incurred for staffing.

No longer need children view museums as distant, strange places to be visited infrequently and hurriedly. Instead, as at the Louis Armstrong Middle School, a museum can become a regular and familiar part of a school and its curriculum. It can be a place where children express themselves creatively both in art and language arts, where they experience art in its many forms (photography, painting, mobiles, and poetry), and where they gain special satisfaction from seeing their work exhibited. Moreover, a museum can be a place that reflects the life of its community, through exhibitions of the works of local artists or exhibitions of the results of community studies. It can become a part of children's lives, encouraging them to explore other art institutions in the community.

Yet More Good Ideas

Decentralizing Chapter 1 Planning

by Helen B. Slaughter, Stephen Powers, and Barbara Benton (March 1986)

Author updates appear in the text in bracketed italics.

In the past, most school districts have organized their compensatory education programs centrally, locating the planning and management unit at the district or project level rather than at the building level. As a result, even effective compensatory programs have often not been well-integrated into the overall effort toward school improvement.

Successful planning for school improvement must include the building-level personnel who will ultimately carry out the school improvement projects. Working on the premise that the involvement of principals in school improvement efforts is the key to providing classroom environments conducive to learning, the Tucson Unified School District began during the 1982-83 school year to restructure its $3 million Chapter 1 program. The aim of this restructuring was to allow principals more flexibility and autonomy in developing and implementing Chapter 1 programs at the building level.

The district involved principals in planning for these changes from the outset. In the spring, the principals assessed the needs of their schools. The Chapter 1 staff provided the principals with technical assistance and inservice training on conducting needs assessments. The principals documented the participation of classroom teachers, specialists, and parents in the needs assessments.

After meeting with their school staffs and parents, the principals of buildings with similar needs met in small groups with Chapter 1 staff members from the central office to explore alternative programs. The Chapter 1 staff

---

Helen B. Slaughter is an associate professor in the College of Education at the University of Hawaii at Manoa, Honolulu. Stephen Powers is a Chapter 1 evaluator for the Tucson (Ariz.) Unified School District, where Barbara Benton is director of instruction and externally funded programs.

members shared with them information on the latest federal guidelines and research findings on program effectiveness. They also addressed the principals' questions about the feasibility of using Chapter 1 funds in new ways. If these questions could not be resolved on the spot, they were forwarded to the state Chapter 1 office.

The principals then returned to their buildings and completed forms that listed, in rank order, the projects they wanted funded through Chapter 1. The principals were not limited to listing existing Chapter 1 projects; they could also propose new projects or suggest modifications of existing projects. To reduce paperwork for principals, the Chapter 1 staff wrote many of the project descriptions — sometimes even for those new projects that had originated in the schools.

After district-level budgetary decisions were made, each school received a copy of its own Chapter 1 application, along with project modification forms. In the spring, the principals could use these materials to further refine a project design; in the fall, they could use the materials to amend a project.

Decentralized planning has several advantages. Principals take more responsibility for the resultant programs and thus work harder to solve problems that arise during the implementation phase. Classroom teachers are more actively involved in the Chapter 1 needs assessment and planning process, which makes them more committed to the success of the programs. Meanwhile, because they are now included in building-level as well as district-level planning, Chapter 1 staff members feel that they play a larger role in improving achievement.

Several new Chapter 1 projects were started in Tucson last year through the activities of principals. One principal proposed an extended-day primary project for low-achievers who were eligible for Chapter 1 funds but who performed too well to be included in the pullout reading and language project conducted during the school day. After this project was started in one school, three other principals used carryover funds to implement similar projects.

[*In 1987-88, the Extended-Day Project is no longer a Chapter 1 project. A new program that has emerged is the Child and Parent Enhancement Program (CAPE) that is home-based and designed for three-year-old children and their parents. The goal of this program is to work with parents and children on home and school readiness skills. Other trends in the Chapter 1 programs are the encouragement of building-level research and greater heterogeneity in the gouping of children.*]

Several Tucson principals were interested in implementing full-day Chapter 1 kindergarten projects, and such projects were ultimately funded at two schools. A third school used Chapter 1 funds to split one kindergarten class into two small groups. Meanwhile, one principal worked with the Chapter 1 staff to design a developmental first-grade language arts package for students who are not ready for more conventional approaches. [*In 1987-88, that program has merged with the regular Chapter 1 program for that grade.*]

In planning Chapter 1 projects, the biggest problem for principals has been the need to submit Chapter 1 budget requests before they know how much supplementary support they can expect from the school district. This unavoidable problem has made planning more difficult.

By decentralizing Chapter 1 program development and implementation, the Tucson Unified School District is better able to deal with local needs while still meeting state and federal guidelines. The decentralization process is still evolving as we begin the fourth program cycle. But it is already clear that the advantages of the process — enthusiasm and commitment, coordination of projects at the building level, and compatibility with modern theories of effective school management — are well worth the effort involved. [*In the 1987-88 school year, the principles of decentralized Chapter 1 planning continue to be applicable to the planning and management of Chapter 1.*]

Connecticut Program Covers Classrooms of Absent Teachers, Provides Tutors

by J. Robert Ford (June 1982)

The traditional system of hiring substitute teachers is inefficient. Substitutes are generally required to take attendance, to announce assignments designated by the absent teacher, and to maintain order. Unfortunately, their ability to carry out even these limited objectives is severely hindered by their transience and their ignorance of a school's procedures.

To address these difficulties, we have developed a new approach at Ellington (Conn.) High School. Since September 1980 we have used the money normally budgeted for substitutes to hire three paraprofessionals instead. This brings our total paraprofessional staff to six.

During the past two school years, these paraprofessionals have covered all supervisory, noninstructional assignments that had previously been handled by teachers. This frees teachers from duties in study halls, the suspension room, the cafeteria, the corridor, and the lavatories. The teachers use their free time to staff resource rooms, where they tutor in their specialties. Each department has a resource room available at certain times, depending on the size of the department and on the teachers' schedules.

We assign teachers from the resource rooms to take attendance and to maintain order in the classrooms of absent teachers. No teaching is required or expected. However, when students realize that the teacher supervising their class will be in the building on the next school day, classroom atmosphere improves appreciably.

Our teacher contract requires faculty members to teach five classes and to cover one supervisory assignment. Under the new plan, time spent in the resource room or in supervising the classes of absent teachers takes the place of more traditional supervisory assignments.

In 1980-81, the first year of the new program, teachers covered classes during 18% of the total time that they were assigned to resource rooms. They used the remaining 82% of the time to tutor students. Teachers gave

---

J. Robert Ford is principal of Ellington (Conn.) High School.

149

such academic assistance 1,644 times. Teachers of mathematics, English, and business education tutored the greatest numbers of students: 856, 331, and 251 times respectively.

During the first half of the 1981-82 school year, students used the resource rooms at a rate almost three times that of the previous year. During the first five months of 1981-82, students sought extra help from teachers in the resource rooms 2,597 times.

Another indication of the program's success is the support it has garnered from teachers, verified through a survey of the high school staff by the Ellington Education Association (the teacher bargaining unit). Teachers wish to continue the program, the survey found.

Our program is no cure-all for the problem of staffing the classrooms of absent teachers. The rate of teacher absences and the size of a school will certainly influence the effectiveness of such a program. However, we find in our high school of 600 students that the program is doubly advantageous: It improves conditions in the classrooms of absent teachers, and it provides tutoring for students who need such extra help.

Update — *Mr. Ford writes that the teacher tutorial program described in this article has been continued without change. It remains popular with students, staff, and parents. Since the article was published in 1982, representatives of a number of school systems have observed the program; but Mr. Ford does not know how many have adopted it.*